How Patriotic is the Patriot Act?

How Patriotic is the Patriot Act?

Freedom Versus Security in the Age of Terrorism

Amitai Etzioni

ROUTLEDGE
New York · London

Published in 2004 by
Routledge
270 Madison Avenue
New York, NY 10016
www.routledge-ny.com

Published in Great Britain by
Routledge
2 Park Square
Milton Park, Abingdon
Oxon, OX14 4RN
www.routledge.co.uk

Routledge is an imprint of the Taylor and Francis Group.
Printed in the United Stated of America on acid-free paper.

10 9 8 7 6 5 4 3

Library of Congress Cataloging-in-Publication Data

Etzioni, Amitai.
    How patriotic is the Patriot Act? : freedom versus security in the age of
terrorism / Amitai Etzioni.
        p. cm.
    Includes bibliographical references and index.
    ISBN 0-415-95047-3 (hardback : alk. paper)
    1. United States. Uniting and Strengthening America by Providing Appropriate
Tools Required to Intercept and Obstruct Terrorism (USA PATRIOT ACT)
Act of 2001. 2. National security—Law and legislation—United States.
3. Internal security—United States. 4. Terrorism—United States. 5. Civil
rights—United States. I. Title.
    KF4850.E899 2004
    345.73'02—dc22

                                                        2004009294

For Jonathan Etzioni, the youngest
member of the growing Etzioni family,
born January 25, 2004.

*"We're not asking for wholesale repeal of the
PATRIOT Act . . . we're saying fix it."*
—Laura Murphy, head of the ACLU Washington, D.C. office

*". . . a state of war is not a blank check for the President
when it comes to the rights of the Nation's citizens."*
—Supreme Court Justice Sandra Day O'Connor

Other Books by Amitai Etzioni

From Empire to Community:
A New Approach to International Relations (2004)

The Common Good (2004)

My Brother's Keeper:
A Memoir and a Message (2003)

The Monochrome Society (2001)

The Limits of Privacy (1999)

The New Golden Rule:
Community and Morality in a Democratic Society (1996)

The Spirit of Community:
The Reinvention of American Society (1993)

The Moral Dimension:
Toward a New Economics (1988)

Capital Corruption:
The New Attack on American Democracy (1984)

An Immodest Agenda:
Rebuilding America before the Twenty-First Century (1983)

Genetic Fix:
The Next Technological Revolution (1973)

The Active Society:
A Theory of Societal and Political Processes (1968)

Political Unification:
A Comparative Study of Leaders and Forces (1965)

Modern Organizations (1964)

A Comparative Analysis of Complex Organizations (1961)

Table of Contents

Acknowledgments

I am indebted to Andrew Volmert, Jason Marsh, Mackenzie Baris, Jared Bloom, Anne Hardenbergh, and Deirdre Mead for extensive research assistance and editorial comments. In preparing these articles, I greatly benefited from comments by Peter Swire, Orin Kerr, Dennis Bailey, Jerry Berman, Marc Dunkelman, Shane Ham, Lara Flint, Joanna McIntosh, Neville Pattinson, Ari Schwartz, and Tom Wolfsohn. Emily Pryor prepared the book for publication.

"How Liberty is Lost" was published as part of a symposium titled "Fallacies in Democracy" in *Society* 40, no. 5 (2003): 44–51.

"Privacy and Security in Electronic Communications" was published in the *Harvard Journal of Law and Technology* 15, no. 2 (spring 2002): 258–90.

"A Case for National ID Cards?" was published as Appendix A in *Creating a Trusted Information Network for Homeland Security: Second Report of the Markle Foundation Task Force* (New York: The Markle Foundation, December 2003).

"The Limits of Nation Building" was published in *International Affairs* 80, no. 1 (January 2004): 1–17.

All articles were modified, extended, and updated.

Introduction

One central thesis of this volume is that the starting point of any reasonable deliberation about our national security is the recognition that we face two profound commitments: protecting our homeland and safeguarding our rights. Those who, in effect, seek to suspend major parts of the Constitution and its Bill of Rights until we win the war against terrorism must realize that this is a long-term war and, hence, provisions that might apply for a very short period, during a dire state of emergency, cannot be applied here. To live for any length of time without the rule of law that makes us what we are is not an option, nor should it be. Equally fallacious are the notions that nothing changed on September 11, 2001, and that the fear of future attacks is merely used by the government to keep the people fearful and willing to yield ever increasing power to the state. There is room for much deliberation as to exactly what must be done and whether there is a need for some limited trade-offs. But the starting point for such an assessment is that we are committed to being both free and secure. True patriots thus realize that one must protect the nation from all enemies, foreign and domestic, and that the essence of what it means to be patriotic is to protect our Constitution and its Bill of Rights with all of our might.

Discussions of matters concerning public affairs are often couched in terms acquired from our legal culture. The implicit assumption is that each side (rarely is there room for more) will state its position like lawyers in court, in the starkest possible terms, drawing on whatever arguments they can marshal, even if these greatly distort the facts and vastly misrepresent the other side. Truth and justice are supposed to arise out of such confrontations between two extreme presentations. I am not confident that this is the best way to run a court system, but surely it is a poor way to form public policies and to debate their merits. But this is the way much of the exceedingly divisive debate over civil rights versus public safety has been conducted.

On the one side, civil libertarians, liberals, and some conservatives (Bob Barr, for instance) make strong, uncompromising cases for liberty. In effect, they severely criticize practically any suggestions made in the name of shoring up our safety, including the antiterrorism measures urged upon the country by the 1996 Downing Commission, as unnecessary invasions of our freedoms. These advocates consider the government (a.k.a. Big Brother), not terror, to be the greatest threat to the preservation of liberty. Senator Patrick Leahy said in November 2001 that "We don't protect ourselves by bending or even shredding our Constitution."[1] And in a *New York Times* op-ed article that same month he claimed that the president "is eroding the very values and principles he seeks to protect, including the rule of law."[2] The public is almost daily exposed to a publication bemoaning "the death of privacy"[3] and the rise of the "surveillance society."[4]

On the other side, the political right characterizes the ACLU and its sister organizations, all of which are generally liberal, as undermining the moral fabric of the country, destroying its social order, and inviting terrorism. Jerry Falwell pointed a finger at "the pagans, and the abortionists, and the feminists, and the gays and the lesbians who are actively trying to make that [sic] an alternative lifestyle, the ACLU, People for the American Way, all of them who have tried to secularize America."[5] Attorney General Ashcroft said, "[T]o those who scare peace-loving people with phantoms of lost liberty, my message is this: your tactics only aid terrorists, for they erode our national unity and diminish our resolve."[6] Harvard professor Ruth Wisse wrote in *Commentary* that her fellow faculty members' concerns after September 11, 2001 centered solely around the potential that the new legislation might intrude upon their freedoms and privacy. She went on to write, "I pray that my life will never depend on the intervention of these moral eunuchs, who have extended a canopy of olive branches over whichever anti-American tyrant chooses to tear the world apart."[7]

Eschewing this vitriolic and polarizing approach, this book takes it for granted that we must shore up our protection from terrorist attacks, especially as these are likely to increase in severity, and that we must vigilantly protect our rights and our free way of life. Only when we have failed to do this will we have done the terrorists' job for them. *It holds then that extremism in the defense of either security or liberty is not a virtue.* Moreover, although to some extent we can reconcile these two claims that we now face, there is a basic tension between them that must be acknowledged and resolved.

A July 18, 2004 *Washington Post* editorial titled "More Patriot Act Games," put it well, and in so doing summarized the approach in this volume, when it pointed to the tendency to polarize the debate about the PATRIOT Act instead of dealing differently with its various components. The editorial stated: ". . . public debate over the law's fate has fallen victim to election-year demagoguery. Critics talk about it as though it were a comprehensive menace, while President Bush and Attorney General John D. Ashcroft often treat skepticism of it as softness in the war on terror." The editorial called instead for an examination of each part of the act on its own merit (or demerit). This is exactly what here is attempted.

Freedom and Security: A Communitarian Perspective

The arguments I advance here draw on a social, philosophical position, known as *responsive communitarianism* (it is also known as new, or political; not to be confused with Asian communitarians or the academic communitarianism of the 1980s). I sometimes serve as a voice for this school.[8] However, there are differences among responsive communitarians and I should make it clear that I write along this line of thinking but strictly as I see it.

A key tenet of responsive communitarianism is that a good society is based on a carefully crafted balance between liberty and social order, and a combination of particularistic (communal) and societywide values and bonds. This school stresses the responsibilities that people have to their families, kin, communities, and societies. These exist above and beyond the universal rights that all individuals command, which is a main focus of liberalism. Communitarianism has clear parallels in the Constitution and our legal tradition and in a number of court cases that have affected the way we live and govern.

Particularly relevant for the issues at hand is the Fourth Amendment. It is not phrased in terms as absolute as the First Amendment. It does not state that Congress "shall make no law allowing search and seizure" or anything remotely like it. It states that there be no *un*reasonable searches. It is one of only two rights-defining amendments that recognize, on the face of it, the importance of taking into account the public interest. Indeed, the courts have long recognized that our right to privacy must be weighed against our need for public safety (and public health). It highlights how unreasonable it is to argue that we should not sacrifice our rights for our security. In fact, it demonstrates that this is a highly misleading way of framing of the issue, just as it would be misleading for someone to argue that we should sacrifice our security to protect our rights. There is a whole range of security enhancing measures that public authorities can take, measures that are reasonable and that do not violate any rights. *No one has a right to never be searched, stopped, fingerprinted, and so on, and hence they cannot lose it.*

But what, then, is reasonable? The law—which often draws on this concept—views this standard as that which an average person, a member of the community, would consider reasonable. There can be no doubt that Americans have an altered sense of that which is reasonable since September 11, 2001. This does not mean that they threw the Bill of Rights out the window. Data presented in Chapter 1 will show that this is hardly the case. However, many Americans do now find some new security measures reasonable that they may well have not embraced before the attacks on September 11. By and large, polling indicates that Americans favor a carefully crafted balance between the two competing claims of security and freedom. Moreover, when the government has deviated from this balance here and resorted to measures that the public has not considered acceptable, public opinion has forced it to retreat and either withdraw or recast most of these measures as we shall see.

The Constitution has always been a living document and it has been adapted to the changing needs of the times. This is evident if one recalls that until the ACLU started to defend those accused of subversion during the 1920s, the First Amendment was hardly a steely protector of free speech. More dramatically, if we were to rely on the unchanging text of the Constitution, then of course we would have no right to privacy, which the Constitution does not even mention; indeed, privacy as a constitutional right, has been fashioned as recently as 1965. If we can create a whole new right out of the penumbra of the Constitution—as the right to privacy was fashioned—then we can surely refashion this and other rights. Such new interpretations are called for not because the nation experienced the most devastating attack on our homeland in its history, but because there are strong reasons to expect that the country will face in the future more and worse attacks.

Unfortunately, societies do not have finely tuned, reliable guidance mechanisms.[9] They have a tendency to oversteer in one direction or the other. Fortunately, in democratic societies, this oversteering is correctable, often although far from always, before we go off the track too far and for too long. Viewed in this way, the Hoover FBI initiated a much needed drive to professionalize the work of law enforcement authorities that were corrupt, partisan, and riddled with nepotism and favoritism in the wake of the Prohibition. However, by 1970 the FBI had infiltrated all kinds of civil rights and politically legitimate but dissenting groups. (As a peacenik, I was on the target list.)[10] It conducted numerous inappropriate wiretaps and other acts of surveillance. J. Edgar Hoover became accountable to no one, as presidents and Congress members feared him because of files that he kept on their personal lives and because he succeeded in building a public myth around himself. In response, the Church Commission introduced numerous limitations on what the FBI could do, and the FBI issued several internal memos that further tied the hands of law enforcement agents.[11] By the end of the 1990s, not rocking the boat, not going near the line that separated the clearly legal from the gray areas was considered a wise way to advance within the organization, with some notable exceptions.[12]

Then came September 11, 2001, and we learned that a major reason why it occurred was that the FBI lacked various powers, its agents feared to act, the Department of Justice kept it on a fairly tight leash, and a fire wall existed between it and the CIA. The USA PATRIOT Act and several other measures that followed, as we shall see, removed many of these restraints. These acts corrected previous overcorrections to prior misconduct. In the process, authorities went too far in the other direction and they are being corrected yet again. To illustrate, following public outcry led by the ACLU and similar organizations, the Justice Department made important clarifications about the originally vague nature of military tribunals to try suspected terrorists. Similarly, Operation TIPS (Terrorist Information and Prevention System), which encouraged Americans to spy on one another, had such frightening implications that it was quickly scrapped. Also scrapped due to privacy concerns was the Computer Assisted Passenger Prescreening System (CAPPS II), which would have allowed government officials to collect personal information about airline passengers in order to identify who may pose as a security risk. Surely, more adjustment will be needed in the future and will in effect take place daily, but we are groping for that middle ground rather than allowing extremists from either side to push us off the road. In the words of Laura Murphy, head of the Washington, D.C. office of the ACLU, "We're not asking for wholesale repeal of the PATRIOT Act . . . we're saying fix it."

The preceding general thesis is examined in some detail in Chapter 2. It provides an overview of the various new security measures that officials have introduced and the ways that they have been modified over the years that have passed since the hurried enactment of the USA PATRIOT Act in the aftermath of September 11, 2001. Chapter 3 zeros in on six measures and examines them much more closely. It concludes that often the issue is not that a given measure violates rights or that it protects rights to the point that security is undermined, but rather that the heart of the matter is how well the application of the new security measures is supervised, overseen, and accounted for.

The discussion then turns, in Chapter 4, to still another specific set of new security measures: those that concern defense from bioterrorism. Here, the questions about to what extent rights can be compromised for national security concerns focus on matters surrounding involuntary isolation or quarantining of people and obligatory vaccinations. The new measures that have been taken, and those that should be taken, to defend the public from attacks with biological agents have a unique feature that makes them of special interest to a communitarian. The reason is that most of the other measures are of little value if there are no new attacks. However, many of the improvements suggested to protect public health by preventing and coping with biological and chemical attacks would serve the nation well even if never used to fight terrorists. For instance, such measures could also deal with the spread of an infectious disease such as SARS, the flu, or AIDS. That is, these measures promote the public health, a major common good, even if they will contribute nothing to national security.

Chapter 5 examines the possibility of issuing national ID cards in an effort to bolster homeland security. Due to the many acts of identity theft and the still graver threats posed by terrorists who are able to operate on U.S. soil through the use of fake driver's licenses, visas and passports, there is a strong need to develop more reliable means of identification. I argue here that the government, in cooperation with private industry, should offer voluntary identification cards that would expedite entry into controlled areas such as airports or even the United States itself.

My analysis in Chapter 6—drawing on the works of many before me—focuses on ways to enhance our security by acting in lands other than our own. In this chapter, I suggest that the neo-conservative rush to democratize nations the world over is an unattainable goal. A much more modest agenda is called for. The implication is not that we should cease to promote human rights, liberty, and democracy in other nations, but rather that we should realize that there are severe limits on how much progress can be made by such promotion. There cannot be a Marshal Plan for major parts of the world, most of which have different social, economic, and political conditions than Germany and Japan had after World War II. We can, however, set into motion forces that in the longer run will move various nations toward regimes that both respect human rights and are less threatening to our security.

One may well disagree about this or that detail of public policy with regard to domestic and foreign affairs as spelled out in the following pages. However, Americans should share the commitment to find a middle course, a third way, between those who are committed to shore up our liberties but who are blind to the needs of public safety, and those who in the name of security never met a right that they were not willing to curtail to give authorities an ever freer hand. A third way between those who are all too confident that they can remake the world in the mold of America and those who want to withdraw from the world and give up on efforts to make the globe a more hospitable place than it is. Charting the middle course may make for less drama than the clash of uncompromising extremist positions, but it is both where reasonable deliberations and moral considerations direct us. It is also the middle ground in which we can find the best ways to keep us free and secure.

I
How Liberty Is Lost

In the wake of numerous changes made in U.S. law and that of many other countries following the September 11 terrorist attack, civil libertarians, libertarians, and many others have raised concerns that the nations involved are sacrificing their liberty to enhance their safety. Civil libertarian organizations such as the American Civil Liberties Union (ACLU) have described the government's penchant toward obtaining new powers after September 11, 2001, as an "insatiable appetite," characterized by government secrecy, a lack of transparency, rejection of equality under the law, and "a disdain and outright removal of checks and balances."[1] Articles in the popular press express similar sentiments. Writing in the *American Prospect*, Wendy Kaminer expressed the fear that by giving the "FBI unchecked domestic spying powers and instead of focusing on preventing terrorism, it will revert to doing what it does best—monitoring, harassing, and intimidating political dissidents and thousands of harmless immigrants."[2] In short, it has been argued that in order to protect ourselves from terrorists, democracy may be endangered, if not lost.

The question, "Under what conditions is democracy undermined?" has been the topic of considerable previous deliberations, especially by those who have studied the fall of the Weimar Republic and the rise of the Nazis in Germany. However, in past decades, much more focus was placed on the question of how to help democracy grow in countries that have had little previous experience with this form of governance (for instance, some former communist nations and a fair number of developing nations), rather than on how democracy might be lost. Given the recent events and claims, the latter question deserves revisiting. This question is particularly germane because if it were true that in order to survive future waves of terrorist attacks (including ones using weapons of mass destruction) we must turn our free societies into garrison states, many members of free societies might well be reluctant to accept such a trade-off.

Fortunately, the empirical basis for such a study of the conditions under which democracy is actually lost is very limited because democracy—once firmly established—has almost never been lost due to internal developments (as distinct from occupation by an invading force). Democracy seems to be an odd plant: it has been very difficult for it to take root, especially in parts of the world where it has not been "naturally" found, but where various efforts have been made to seed it. Once it buds, it often faces great difficulties and frequently dies on the vine, or at least suffers numerous setbacks before it grows properly. But after it firmly takes root, it tends to withstand numerous challenges well and is rarely lost. Indeed, only one example of democracy lost comes to mind—the already-mentioned Weimar Republic—and it is arguable whether democracy was even well established there. Other cases in point may be found in Latin America.

Before the discussion proceeds, a word on definition. If one defines "democracy" very lightly, such as the holding of regular elections, one finds that none of the preceding statements hold true. Elections are held all over the world, including in nations in which there is only one political party, one candidate, a legislature that rubber-stamps whatever the government proposes, a press controlled by the government, and individual rights that are not respected. Such "democracies" come and go, at the whim of the military or some other power elite. Democracy, here, is taken to mean a polity in which there are regular, institutionalized changes in power, in line with the preferences of the people freely expressed. It entails a whole fabric of institutions: two or more political parties, some measure of checks and balances among the various branches of the government (although, of course, these may differ from the U.S. setup), courts that effectively protect individual rights, and a free press. While some scholars draw important conceptual distinctions between liberal (rights-based) polities and democratic ones, and others focus on the definition of liberty, here we treat all of these as key elements of a democratic polity. To remind the reader of this fact, I use the phrase "constitutional democracy;" our democracy is ensconced in a framework of rights that are not subject to majority rule.

The Slippery Slope Hypothesis

The civil libertarian's narrative about how democracies are lost is basically as follows. First, the government, in the name of national security or some other such cause, trims some rights, which raises little alarm at the time (e.g., the massive detention of Japanese Americans during World War II). Then a few other rights are curtailed (e.g., the FBI spies on civil rights groups and peace activists during the 1960s). Soon, more rights are lost and gradually the entire institutional structure on which democracy rests tumbles down the slope with nobody able to stop it.

If one fully embraces this argument, one cannot in good conscience support any significant adjustments in the ways we interpret the Constitution, its Bill of Rights, the powers allotted to public authorities, and other key features of a democratic polity. If one fears setting foot on the slope because he may end up on his backside at the lower end of the slope, there is only one alternative: to remain frozen at the top, opposed to all changes. When Katie Corrigan, legislative counsel with the ACLU's Washington office, testified before Congress, she noted that the ACLU has supported some post-September 11, 2001, changes, including the fortification of cockpit doors, matching baggage with passengers, and limiting the number of carry-on bags passengers may bring on planes,[4] a rather limited list.

By contrast, I argue that one is able to make notches in the slope. In other words, before setting foot on it, one needs to mark how far he is willing to go and what is unacceptable in order to avoid slipping to a place one is not willing and ought not to go.[5] A detailed examination of the changes introduced after September 11, 2001 in the United States shows that some of them are reasonable (e.g., roving wire tapes) and others are quite unacceptable (e.g., the military tribunals as originally conceived).[6] The distinction between these changes suggests that rather than refusing to adjust, we need to examine more closely the various new measures that are being advanced. Indeed, very few would seek to leave the Constitution as originally formulated, according to which non-Europeans do not count as full persons, there is no right to privacy, and free speech is much less protected than post-1920 interpretations (led by the ACLU to its credit) made it. In short, changes in the ways we view individual rights do not signify the end of a democratic form of government. Indeed, as I shall try to highlight in the next section, the relationship runs the other way around: *when democratic institutions and policies do not provide an adequate response to new challenges, they are undermined.*

The Weimar Hypothesis

There is an immense literature on the question of what led to the collapse of the Weimar Republic and the rise of Nazi Germany, all of which contain numerous different interpretations of that part of history.[7] It is well beyond the scope of this study to try to sort out these differences. For the purposes at hand, it suffices to cull out one hypothesis, which can be further examined in light of recent developments and data. The hypothesis is that the Weimar Republic lost its legitimacy and opened the door to a tyrannical government due to its woefully insufficient responses to major public needs.

Following the defeat of Germany in World War I, the people's pride was already shaken. People felt threatened when defeat in the war was followed by massive unemployment and runaway hyperinflation, leading to what historian Peter Fritzsche calls "extraordinary hardship[s]"[8] and "disastrous economic and political conditions."[9] The Weimar Republic's response was weakened by its difficulties in forming coalitions among its "superabundance of political parties,"[10] corruption, and scandals.[11] The "growing number and severity of the problems confronting the German nation were largely due to the inefficiency of the government,"[12] finds Theodore Abel, who also lists "discontent within the existing social order"[13] as the first factor contributing to the rise of the Nazi movement. He notes that discontent was expressed by people blaming the government for their problems.[14] Overall, "the Weimar system has enormous weaknesses," posits Kurt Sontheimer.[15]

Other scholars, for instance Sheri Berman, point to similar reasons the republic collapsed. She argues that although the Weimar Republic had an active civil society, its weak political institutions and structures sharpened divisions in German society and "obstructed meaningful participation in public life."[16] Likewise, Arthur van Riel and Arthur Schram note that the elected national assembly was unable to respond effectively to economic challenges and that "any struggle for political reform was viewed as a threat to the delicate equilibrium of political and economic interests."[17] Other historians have made similar observations. The inefficiency of democracy and the difficulty of forming a coalition have been highlighted by Fritz Stern, who also argued that "as the economy faltered and the government was unable to react to the economic and political problems, voters turned their back on the Weimar Republic."[18] As a result of the lack of responsiveness, "too many Germans did not regard it as a legitimate regime," writes E. J. Feuchtwanger in *From Weimar to Hitler*[19] (although he notes the other numerous factors that contributed to the republic's demise). Thus, according to these as well as still other scholars, the Weimar Republic did not respond effectively—both economically and politically—to its citizens' major needs in the face of crises, and thus it lost its legitimacy.[20]

Thus, there is good reason to believe that inaction in the face of threats, not excessive action, killed the Weimar Republic. In short, when democracies do not work, they open themselves to tyrannies.

Post-September 11 Lessons

Did our constitutional democracy lose support after September 11, 2001; and if it did, due to what factors? The data cited next suggest that during the immediate period after the attack, when the public was most concerned about its safety (fearing additional attacks from sleeper terrorist cells on short order), people were most willing to support a strong government, including one that would set aside many basic individual rights.

However, in the subsequent period, as the government did take numerous and varying measures to enhance public safety and no new attacks occurred, the public gradually restored its commitment to the rights centered, democratic regime. And as the government vigorously enacted measures to protect the public, the public's support for constitutional democracy was reaffirmed. That is, the U.S. experience in the months following September 11, 2001, helps support the suggested hypothesis by providing a case with a profile opposite that of the Weimar one. *When the government reacted firmly to a major challenge, support for constitutional democracy was sustained rather than undermined.*

The Rise and Fall of Public Fears

To put the hypothesis that is being explored here in semiformal terms, it might be said that we seek to assess whether the size of a challenge (in this instance the September 11 terrorist attacks) minus the impact of new measures undertaken to enhance public safety will correlate with the extent to which the public will support a rights-based, constitutional democracy. For the purposes at hand, no distinction is made as to whether the public's concerns are realistic, overblown, or underestimating the danger. (We know from crime studies that the public's fear of crime and the actual level of crimes do not necessarily go hand in hand.) The reason for this approach is that democracy will be endangered if the public's fears rise above a certain level, regardless of whether or not these concerns are realistic. The same holds for safety measures. If putting armed guards in airports adds little to public safety but helps to reassure the public, then armed guards will serve to reduce anxiety and help undergird public support for our form of government.

Airline Traffic: Behavioral Data

A reasonable measure of the initial scope of the public's safety concerns and the extent to which it declined after September 11, 2001, is provided by statistics on domestic airline traffic within the United States. This examination is based on behavioral data that is considered more reliable than attitudinal data, to which I will have to turn shortly. Airline traffic fell precipitously in the period immediately following the attack, and very gradually it recovered.

Prior to September 11, 2001, airlines were experiencing a slight increase of a little less than one percent in airline travelers over the year 2000; in August 2001, passengers boarding flights increased by 3.1 percent over the previous year (a year-high 56.4 million passengers boarded U.S. carriers for domestic flights in August 2001; 54.5 million did so in August 2000).[21] In September 2001 (which includes the 10 days before the attack), enplanements dropped 34 percent from September 2000 (when 46.4 million passengers boarded planes, compared to the 30.5 million who did so during the month of the attacks, when airports across the country were shut down).[21]

Traffic began a slow but steady increase during the remainder of the year, although enplanements remained considerably less than what they were during the same months in the year 2000. In October, 2001 air carriers experienced 21 percent fewer enplanements over the previous year (a decrease from 51 million to 40.3 million). As the highly traveled holiday months approached, the drop in enplanements continued to recede. In November 2001 there were 18 percent fewer enplanements than during the same month in the previous year (a decrease from 50 million to 41 million) and December 2001 saw a 13 percent decrease over the 2000 holiday season (from 47 million to 41 million).[22] By 2004, airline travel had returned to its pre-September 11, 2001 levels.

The first two months of the year 2002 followed the same pattern, showing people slowly but steadily returning to air travel. January 2002 enplanements were down 13.0 percent compared to 2001 (a decrease from 44 million to 38.1 million), and February 2002 saw 9 percent fewer enplanements compared to February, 2001 (a decrease from 43 million to 39 million).[23]

In short, as numerous new airline safety measures were introduced, a potential attack (by a so-called shoe-bomber) was successfully foiled, and no others took place, the public's confidence in airline travel was gradually being restored.

Commitment to Constitutional Democracy: Attitudes

One can see a baseline of sorts in the following data on perceptions about personal freedoms (Table 1). A year before the September 11 attacks, 54 percent of Americans were not concerned that the government threatens their own personal rights and freedoms; while two months after the attacks, the figure rose to 67 percent, encompassing two-thirds of all Americans.[24] (By that time several measures to enhance safety had been introduced

Table 1 Governmental Threats to Personal Rights and Freedoms

Do you think the government threatens your own personal rights and freedoms, or not?			
	YES	NO	DON'T KNOW
November 2001	30	67	3
June 2000[a]	46	54	—[b]

Source: National Public Radio/Kaiser/Kennedy School Poll on Civil Liberties, October 31–November 12, 2001.
[a] National Public Radio/Kaiser/Kennedy School of Government.
[b] Less than one percent.

and public fears began to subside. Regrettably, no data is available for the same question immediately after the attack.)

When people were asked explicitly, "Would you be willing to give up some of the liberties we have in this country in order for the government to crack down on terrorism, or not?," their responses tell the same story. Shortly after the bombing of the Murrah Federal Building in Oklahoma City in April 1995, a hefty majority (59 percent) favored giving up some liberties. After a month, the numbers began to subside to 52 percent, only to zoom to about 66 percent of Americans following September 11, 2001.[25]

The same sentiments are revealed in another poll that asked, "What concerns you most right now? That the government will fail to enact strong, new antiterrorism laws, or that the government will enact new antiterrorism laws which excessively restrict the average person's civil liberties?" While 44 percent were concerned that the government would enact laws that restrict civil liberties in 1995, about one-third (34 percent) expressed such reservations in September 2001.[26]

The willingness of people to give up rights in order to fight terrorism, and their perception of whether or not they will need to give up some of their own rights, is also tied to their level of fear. As Table 2 shows, a clear majority (59 percent) of Americans were willing to give up some liberties after what was, in retrospect, a small attack, the bombing of the federal building in Oklahoma City in April 1995. When the same question was asked a mere month later, people already had begun to calm down, and their willingness to support reductions of liberty declined to 52 percent. After the 2001 attacks on America, two-thirds of Americans were willing to sacrifice some liberty to fight terrorism. (When the question was worded differently, the percentage was even higher—78 percent.)

Questions about "necessity" instead of willingness to give up liberties (Table 3) reveal a similar pattern. More than six in ten Americans agreed that it was necessary to give up some rights immediately after

Table 2 Willingness to Give up Civil Liberties

DATE	QUESTION	WILLING	NOT WILLING	DON'T KNOW/ NO OPINION
April 1995[a]	Would you be willing to give up some of the liberties we have in this country in order for the government to crack down on terrorism, or not?	59	24	10
May 1995[a]	Would you be willing to give up some of the liberties we have in this country in order for the government to crack down on terrorism, or not?	52	41	7
August 1996[b]	Would you be willing to give up some civil liberties if that were necessary to curb terrorism in this country, or not?	58	23	6
September 2001[a]	Would you be willing to give up some of the liberties we have in this country in order for the government to crack down on terrorism, or not?	66	24	7
January– March 2002[c]	You are now more willing to give up certain freedoms to improve safety and security than you were before September 11th.	78	22	—

Source: [a]ABC News/*Washington Post* Poll, September 11 2001.
[b]*Los Angeles Times Poll,* August 3–August 6, 1996. This poll was conducted a few weeks after the explosion of TWA flight 800 and the bombing at Centennial Olympic Park during the 1996 Summer Olympics in Atlanta. The poll also contained the response "it depends," chosen by 13 percent of respondents (which is not included in Table 2).
[c]Gallup Poll, January 28–March 22, 2002. Responses to the question included "strongly agree" (29.5 percent), "agree" (48.8 percent), "disagree" (13.6 percent), and "strongly disagree" (8.1 percent).

September 11, 2001. Two months later, the number fell to a bit more than five out of ten Americans.

Asked about specific measures, the picture is consistent: as fear subsides, support for safety, even at the cost of liberty, remained high (following warnings about more attacks, including ones with dirty bombs and bioterror agents, were standard diet), fears declined over time and so did public support for all of the ten specific measures the public was

Table 3 Necessity to Give up Liberties

DATE	QUESTION	NECESSARY	NOT NECESSARY	DON'T KNOW
September 2001[a]	In order to curb terrorism in this country, do you think it will be necessary for the average person to give up some liberties or not?	61	33	6
November 2001[b]	In order to curb terrorism in this country do you think it will be necessary for the average person to give up some rights and liberties, or do you think we can curb terrorism without the average person giving up rights and liberties?	51*	46*	3
November 2001[b]	Do you think you will have to give up some of your **OWN** rights and liberties in order to curb terrorism, or not?	58**	39**	3

Source: [a]*Los Angeles Times* Poll, September 13–14, 2002.
[b]National Public Radio/Kaiser/Kennedy School Poll on Civil Liberties, October 31, 2001–November 12, 2001.
Notes: *Responses include "necessary for the average person to give up some rights and liberties" and "we can curb terrorism without the average person giving up rights and liberties."
**Responses include "yes" and "no".

asked about. Indeed, on seven out of the ten measures, more than two-thirds of Americans were initially willing to sacrifice the specific rights listed.

When the same issue was raised in a different manner, the results were similar. Table 5 shows that the percentage of Americans who held that the government went too far in restricting civil liberties to fight terrorism remained consistently small, and the percentage of those who believed that the government did not go far enough declined somewhat as America experienced no new attacks and numerous new safety measures were introduced.

In response to overarching questions (such as, "Overall, how confident do you feel that U.S. law enforcement will use its expanded

Table 4 Law Enforcement and Civil Liberties

Here are some increased powers of investigation that law enforcement agencies might use when dealing with people suspected of terrorist activity, which would also affect our civil liberties. For each, please say if you would favor or oppose it.

		FAVOR	OPPOSE	NOT SURE/ DECLINE TO ANSWER
Expanded undercover activities to penetrate groups under suspicion	Sept. 2001	93	5	1
	March 2002	88	10	2
Stronger documents and physical security checks	Sept. 2001	93	6	1
	March 2002	89	9	2
Stronger document and physical security checks for access to government and private buildings	Sept. 2001	92	7	1
	March 2002	89	10	1
Use of facial-recognition technology to scan for suspected terrorists at various locations and public events	Sept. 2001	86	11	2
	March 2002	81	17	2
Issuance of a secure I.D. technique for persons to access government and business computer systems, to avoid disruptions	Sept. 2001	84	11	4
	March 2002	78	16	6
Closer monitoring of banking and credit card transactions, to trace funding sources	Sept. 2001	81	17	2
	March 2002	72	25	2
Adoption of a national I.D. system for all U.S. citizens	Sept. 2001	68	28	4
	March 2002	59	37	5
Expanded camera surveillance on streets and in public places	Sept. 2001	63	35	2
	March 2002	58	40	2
Law enforcement monitoring of Internet discussions in chat rooms and other forums	Sept. 2001	63	32	5
	March 2002	55	41	4
Expanded government monitoring of cell phones and e-mail, to intercept communications	Sept. 2001	54	41	4
	March 2002	44	51	4

Source: Harris Poll, March 13–19, 2002 and Harris Poll, September 19–24, 2001.

Table 5 Government Excess in Restricting Civil Liberties

Based on what the Bush Administration has done so far and is proposing to do in response to terrorism, do you think they are going too far in restricting civil liberties in this country, not far enough, or are handling this situation just about right?

	TOO FAR	NOT FAR ENOUGH	JUST ABOUT RIGHT	DON'T KNOW
September 2001	12	23	59	6
November 2001	11	14	72	3
February 2002	8	17	72	3

Source: Newsweek Poll, 31 January–1 February 2002.

surveillance powers in what you would see as a proper way, under the circumstances of terrorist threats?"), we see the beginning of a shift. There is a decline in those who are very confident law enforcement will use such powers properly, which is much less problematic than a significant increase in those who are not confident at all would be. While in March, the percentage of people who felt "very confident" fell to almost one-third of what it was in September (from 34 percent to 12 percent), those who were "not confident at all" increased by a mere two percentage points (from 4 percent to 6 percent), well within the margin of error for such polls.[27]

All in all, as far as one can rely on attitudinal data that varies according to how the question is phrased, the data support the thesis that the higher the fear, the greater the willingness to curtail liberty to protect safety. And that as new safety measures are introduced, and no new attacks occur—when the government's response seems effective—fear subsides and support for democracy beings to increase again. The fact that the support for strong anti-terrorist measures remains high reflects the fact that all of the data was collected within a short period after of the attack and under frequent warnings about immanent attacks, new threats, and so on. The thesis would lead one to expect that if the panic subsides some more, the proportion of those supporting a curtailment of rights will further decline. This may seem obvious but it surely is not so obvious to those who hold that democracy is lost by introducing new safety measures that entail some curtailment of rights. These are core elements of what protects the public and reassures it.[28]

Some critics argue that the frequent alarms are meant to keep the public mobilized in support of the war against terrorism. Actually, more and more people are critical of the numerous changes in status from yellow to orange and back again. Indeed, in the period in which there were numerous alarms, public support for security measures declined. That is, it seems that the public measures its safety less by changes in color codes and more by the number of Americans killed by terrorists in the homeland. There have not been any thus far since the September 11 terrorist attacks; and as long as that continues, the public is expected to feel safer and more concerned with rights than with new security measures.

Crime Rates and Liberty

Beyond the scope of this presentation is another relevant source of data: the correlation between public support for "tough" elected officials and law enforcement personnel who favor restrictive and punitive policies that entail curbing individual liberties. Some informal evidence to this effect is available for the mid-1990s.

Following a series of high-profile violent crimes, including a rampage killing five passengers on a Long Island railroad car and several murders of European tourists in Florida, the public became highly fearful of violent crime and sought get-tough measures. In the mid-1990s, the public cited crime as the biggest problem facing the country (19 percent), with an additional two percent identifying guns as the biggest problem, followed by the economy (14 percent) and unemployment and jobs (12 percent).[29] In 1996 crime and drugs were identified as the biggest problem by nearly a quarter of respondents.[30] In contrast, four years earlier, in January 1992, 54 percent of Americans cited economic issues as the most important issue facing the country, while only two percent cited guns or violence.[31]

In the mid-1990s, Americans overwhelmingly favored treating juveniles who commit violent crimes the same way as adults, as opposed to more leniently (by nearly a three-to-one margin).[32] They also supported more extreme measures such as caning, following American Michael Fay's such punishment in Singapore for vandalism. A 1994 poll shows that less than half of Americans felt that caning is too harsh a punishment for assault (44 percent), robbery (48 percent), and drug dealing (36 percent).[33] Nearly 60 percent of Americans favored the "surgical or chemical castration of men repeatedly convicted of rape or child molesting."[34]

During this same time period, demagogues advocated "street justice" and "shoot first, ask questions later." Former Los Angeles Police Chief Daryl Gates publicly made comments to this effect. For instance, at a news conference about the rioting that occurred after the beating of Rodney King by Los Angeles police officers, Gates was quoted as saying, "Clearly that night we should have gone down there and shot a few people. In retrospect, that's what we should have done. We should have blown a few heads off. And maybe your television cameras would have seen that and maybe that would have been broadcast and maybe, just maybe, that would have stopped everything. I don't know. But certainly we had the legal right to do that."[35] That wasn't the only time Gates made such comments. A few years later, Gates stated, "No matter how use you that club, people are going to criticize."[36] Law enforcement personnel were not alone in expressing their support for "street justice." Other public officials, including legislators, expressed similar views. For example, in 1995 a former member of the Georgia State Assembly introduced a bill (which garnered support, but failed to become law) dubbed "shoot first, ask questions later," which would have allowed homeowners to shoot intruders in their homes.[37]

As the decade came to a close, these sentiments faded away to some degree. A poll conducted in 2000 shows the change in the public's perception of crime. The percentage of those who believed crime in the country was "very bad" or "bad" fell from 90 percent in 1996 to 80 percent in 2000.[38] Even more to the point, among those who felt crime was a problem in the country, less than one-quarter (23 percent) characterized crime as "very bad" or "bad" in their own community in 2000, as compared to the almost one-third (31 percent) who characterized crime as "bad" or "very bad" in 1996.[39] Polls conducted in the late 1990s also showed that people believed there was less crime in their neighborhoods. (In 1998, 48 percent of Americans thought there was less crime in their area than a year ago.)[40] Also, in the latter half of the decade, fewer people believed that crime in the country had increased over the previous year. (In 1998, 52 percent of Americans thought crime increased in the country over the previous year, as compared to 64 percent who thought crime increased in 1997, and 87 percent who thought crime increased in 1993.)[41]

By the end of the 1990s, as public authorities succeeded in curbing violent crime, fear of crime subsided and there was less talk of get-tough, extralegal measures and less support for harsh but legal measures. By the end of the 1990s and in the year 2000, when polls showed that the public perceived crime as less of a problem, the statistics on violent crime corroborated their feelings. For instance, in 1998 there were 1.5 million violent crime offenses,[42] and by the year 2000 offenses decreased even further to 1.4 million,[43] a stark contrast with the much larger number of offenses in the mid-1990s (1.9 million violent crime offenses in 1994 and 1.8 million in 1995.[44]) And as crimes and the fear of crime subsided, the public has been less willing to tolerate police chiefs who openly championed authoritarian methods to curb crime. None are left in any major American city.

Conclusion

To the extent that one can draw conclusions from the evidence at hand—some of it being historical, some behavioral, some anecdotal, and some attitudinal—it seems to support the thesis that democracy is endangered not when strong measures are taken to enhance safety, to protect and reassure the public, but when these measures are not taken. In short, the "correlation" between strong safety measures and democracy is just the opposite of what civil libertarians argue: it is positive rather than negative. This, of course, does not mean that any and all new safety measures are needed, but that, in general, effective enhancement of safety (and more generally, those measures that respond to public needs) is crucial for democracy to be sustained. Once safety is restored, the measures can be gradually rolled back, without endangering public support for constitutional democracy.

2
AN OVERVIEW OF SECURITY MEASURES

A responsible examination of new homeland protection policies finds that they are not all cut from one constitutional, legal, or ethical cloth. They are not all equally "reasonable"; they do not all have the same merit from a national security viewpoint, nor do they raise the same level of concern about their effects on our rights. Several were vastly overdue when they were finally enacted in the wake of September 11, 2001; several are quite reasonable; some raise troubling questions; and at least one major one has yet to be introduced. One may well disagree on any of my specific evaluations of the various new security measures. What I am keen to illustrate, however, is an approach that neither condemns wholesale nor embraces all that the government does in the name of homeland protection. Rather, I seek to assess each measure while keeping in mind the communitarian call for a carefully crafted balance between rights and the common good, particularly national security. Moreover, as new information becomes available about how measures are appropriately and effectively used—or abused—this evaluation may well change. This is how they have fared thus far.

Overdue Measures

Several new safety measures are bringing the law in line with technological developments, an updating that should have been carried out well before September 11, 2001. I discuss some of these at length in the following chapters; here they are only briefly mentioned for the purpose of providing an overview. The most important of these changes involves a law little known before the terrorist attacks, the Foreign Intelligence Surveillance Act (FISA), enacted in the far away days of 1978.[1] FISA provides guidelines under which a federal agent can obtain authorization to conduct surveillance for "foreign intelligence purposes." These purposes include protecting us from acts of foreign powers or their agents (such as terrorists)[2] within the United States, not just of foreigners, but also of Americans.[3] A major tool of surveillance is wiretaps.

Historically, wiretaps were limited to a *given phone*, say to the one in the suspect's home or office, because that was the means of communication most people used in those technologically backward days. Over the past decades, people acquired multiple phones, cell phones, and e-mail accounts, but federal officials engaged in surveillance under FISA could not follow suspects as they changed the instruments they were using—unless they wanted to get a new court order for each communication device. The USA PATRIOT Act, enacted in October 2001, overcame this limitation by amending the existing FISA law to allow what is called "roving surveillance authority"[4]—making it legal for agents to follow one suspect, whatever instrument he or she uses. Unless one holds that terrorists are entitled to benefit from new technologies but law enforcement is not entitled to catch up, this is an overdue and reasonable measure.[5]

Moreover, despite claims by the critics that such surveillance orders are all too common, actually—given that nearly 40 million foreigners visit the United States each year, according to the Commerce Department[6]—rather few such orders have been authorized. Little more than 1,000 applications for such orders were made in 2002 before the FISA court, and in 2003, that number still did not exceed 1,727.[7]

Before September 11, 2001, the regulations that allowed public authorities to record or trace e-mail were interpreted by Department of Justice lawyers as requiring court orders from several jurisdictions through which e-mail messages travel.[8] This was the case because in the old days phone lines were local and hence to tap a phone local authorization sufficed. In contrast, e-mail messages zoom by a variety of routes. Now, thanks to the USA PATRIOT Act, national tracing and recording orders are permitted under FISA.[9] That is, law enforcement authorities have finally been allowed to catch up with the particular technological features of e-mail. Anybody who sees a civil rights violation here should have his or her vision checked.

Few changes in the laws and regulations after the 2001 assault on America have raised more ire from civil libertarians than new Department of Justice guidelines, introduced in May 2002, that permit the FBI to conduct surveillance on political and religious organizations.[10] The new guidelines state, "For the purpose of detecting or preventing terrorist activities, the FBI is authorized to visit any place and attend any event that is open to the public, on the same terms and conditions as members of the public generally."[11] Civil libertarians are up in arms because more than a generation ago the FBI infiltrated some civil rights and fringe groups (such as the Ku Klux Klan and the Black Panthers). But today we have a very different FBI from the one run by J. Edgar Hoover. In the reforms that followed in the mid-1970s, the FBI was prohibited from simply attending a public event or going to a public space to observe the goings-on there, even if these events were open to all comers, unless they were investigating a specific crime.[12]

As a result, we lived in an absurd situation in which a terrorist cell could meet in a place of worship without any concern that their plotting might be overheard by public authorities.[13] Or, if they called their cell a "political club," they knew they could not be the subject of surveillance. Far from a theoretical issue, several mosques have been a major ground for recruiting terrorists. For instance, scores of people living in Britain were recruited in mosques in London to fight with the Taliban and some of the September 11 hijackers were recruited in a mosque in Hamburg, according to German security sources.[14] Since the September 11 terrorist attacks, several mosques have been investigated for links to terrorism,[15] including a 2002 federal grand jury investigation of two mosques in the Seattle area and a 2003 investigation of two mosques in the St. Louis area.[16] Not allowing terrorists a secure haven seems reasonable. However, the same does not hold when the FBI spies on civil rights groups and others who peacefully protest the war, globalization, or anything else when there is no link to terrorism. Newspapers have reported that such spying is taking place.[17] If this is true, it constitutes a prime example of violating rights without any contribution to national security.

The Department of Justice is abusing the special powers encompassed in the USA PATRIOT Act not only to catch terrorists, but also to pursue individuals suspected of distributing drugs and stealing identities, among other crimes.[18] The same powers also landed a lovelorn 20 year old woman in a federal prison for two years for endangering a "mass transit system" because she left threatening notes on a cruise ship during a family vacation in hopes of getting the ship to turn around so that she could be reunited with her boyfriend.[19] These recent moves by the Department of Justice are alarming even to centrists like myself because, in effect, they treat all Americans as if they are terrorist suspects.

It is well known that treating various kinds of offenses differently, according to their severity, is at the foundation of our legal and moral code. We do not condemn people to a lifetime in jail for jaywalking. According to the same code, we also calibrate the powers that we grant the government in dealing with suspects not yet convicted of anything. For example, judges deny bail to those who are suspected of major crimes; at the same time, those who are suspected of having committed lesser crimes are free to wait at home until their case is heard (even if they are as likely to flee as the first group). One can argue that some of these categories should be updated, but to undermine them all by treating almost everybody as if they were suspected of terrorism is utterly unacceptable.

Before the September 11 terrorist attack, a Chinese wall separated intelligence agencies such as the CIA and NSA and law enforcement agencies—above all, the FBI. As Attorney General Ashcroft put it in his July 2002 testimony before the Senate, "a criminal investigator examining a terrorist attack could not coordinate with an intelligence officer investigating the same suspected terrorists."[20] He also stated that "barriers between agencies broke down cooperation. Compartmentalization hampered coordination."[21] Michael Hayden, the director of the NSA, informed a recent meeting of the Council on Foreign Relations in Washington, D.C. that his staff members were repeatedly drilled in not sharing "raw information" (which included names and addresses and other identifying marks) with anybody.

Since the September 11 terrorist attack, the government has largely removed the walls separating various intelligence and law enforcement agencies. A major factor was a 2002 court ruling that permitted information sharing between intelligence agents and criminal investigators under FISA.[22] And a new culture is being fostered, one that puts a premium on collaboration where it was earlier avoided. Turf battles have not disappeared, but there is a growing awareness that the enemy is not the other agency, but rather bin Laden and his agents. Attorney General Ashcroft is rhapsodic about the new culture, describing it as one that is "capable of adaptation, secured by accountability, nurtured by cooperation, built on coordination, and rooted in our Constitutional liberties."[23] Even without such Hollywood music in the background, it is good to know that now, as a rule, the left hand is allowed to know what the right hand has found out.

Reasonable Measures Post-September 11, 2001

Officials have introduced some measures that arguably were not needed before September 11, 2001. Prominent among them is a tracking system of those who come to study in the United States. Before the September 11 terrorist attack, the United States did not check whether those who came into the country for a defined period of time, say on a student visa, left at the end of that period. Many did not leave, but there was no way of knowing how many there were, who they were, and above all what they were doing. Actually, Congress mandated a partial tracking system with a mouthful of a name, the Student and Exchange Visitor Information System (SEVIS), as far back as 1996 as part of the Illegal Immigration Reform and Immigrant Responsibility Act.[24] But because of widespread opposition from colleges and civil libertarians, Congress did not implement it through an often used device: no funds were appropriated[25] until the passage of the USA PATRIOT Act.[26] The new student tracking system, which is Internet based, requires colleges to verify whether someone from Saudi Arabia, for example, who came to study English at Reed College, did not show up (and hence is in violation of the terms of his visa and may instead be taking flying lessons in Florida). The system was initially plagued with technical difficulties (e.g., when many colleges accessed it, the computer system slowed to a crawl), procedural problems (e.g., to participate a college must be certified by the INS,[27] and some schools had to wait awhile to receive that approval), and political opposition (e.g., several deans of students complained that they were being made to spy for the government).[28] Colleges were also mindful that foreign students often pay full tuition and they feared scaring the students away.

Given that several of the hijackers came to the United States on the pretense that they would study here, and given that there are large numbers of students from the same countries where the terrorists originated, the tracking system is fully justified. The system has been up and running since August 1, 2003, and has largely been debugged. The bureaucratic burdens it entails are generally minimal and the scrutiny involved falls upon people who are not Americans and who came here out of their free will, with the advance knowledge that they will be tracked. Indeed, some kind of tracking system is in place in many democracies. For instance, in EU countries, people who immigrate or visit for longer periods from overseas, or non-citizens who relocate within the country, are required to register with the local police within 30 days.[29] One form or another of tracking is needed so that security forces can do their job.

The most important change in law enforcement since September 11, 2001 is that the FBI, having been instructed by its director, Robert Mueller,[30] and the White House,[31] has shifted focus and procedure from prosecution to prevention, from collecting information after a crime has been committed to preventing terrorist attacks from taking place. The reason the shift is so portentous is that while prosecution deals with suspects, prevention often entails stirring up the pot on the assumption that somewhere in it is something that needs to be disturbed. That is, a considerable number of people who are not suspected of anything will be put through some kind of a wringer in order to try to throw off some terrorist preparation, which authorities fear might be taking place, involving some members of that group.

Thus, in late 2001, per instructions from the Department of Justice, U.S. Attorneys Offices throughout the nation sent letters to about 5,000 men from countries in which Al Qaeda is present or active and who had entered the United States on non-immigrant visas, that is, on work, tourist, or student visas.[32] They were asked to present themselves at FBI offices for interviews. The purpose of these interviews was to find out if the men had information the government might use in thwarting future attacks. Also, to be frank, it is fair to assume that there were some bad seeds among these men, and that interviews might help ferret them out or scare them into leaving the country. In March 2002, Attorney General Ashcroft reported that these interviews were productive. They "provided us with a number of leads which we think to be very important, and helped us establish relationships with individuals in a number of communities in this country that can be helpful to us in terms of information."[33] The government cast a similar dragnet in 2003 when, according to the Justice Department, the FBI interviewed nearly 10,000 Iraqis in the United States.[34]

Some may wonder what the issue is. Why should the government not interview people? However, these investigations entail inviting thousands of innocent people—who, to reiterate, no one claims are suspected of anything—to be interrogated in an FBI office, which is not the way most people like to spend an afternoon. Moreover, a Department of Justice official explained privately that if someone refuses to be interviewed voluntarily or simply does not show up, he would become a suspect and might well be brought in for interrogation.

These are not measures the United States would have taken in normal times. They are a price we must pay for our enhanced security. We simply cannot wait until we are hit before we act. But, it is a far from trivial price.

Troubling Measures

Other new measures do raise difficult questions. Some of these have already been carefully recalibrated. Others have been largely abandoned. Still others, which our security does command, should be subject to enhanced accountability along the lines spelled out in Chapter 3.

Military Tribunals

There is a clear need to avoid disclosing our sources and methods in open court. Indeed, there have been several cases in which we let American spies bargain down their sentences only so they would plead guilty and we would not have to take them to open court.[35] Terrorists should not benefit from threatening us by demanding public trials. At the same time, when the White House initially announced in November 2001 that civilians might be tried before military tribunals, the procedures to be used were vague. They seemed to imply that a death penalty could be imposed by a mere majority of the members of the tribunal and that there would be no opportunity for appeal. However, in March 2002, the Pentagon clarified the matter, announcing that a unanimous verdict will be required for the death penalty, that the press may cover most proceedings, that defendants will be eligible for military lawyers at government expense, and that suspects will be presumed innocent until proven guilty. The rules do not provide a process for independent appeals, although appeals are possible through the military.[36] These are welcome clarifications. Still, military tribunals should be used as sparingly as possible.

Enemy Combatants

Another particularly troubling measure is the president's ability to declare an American citizen an "enemy combatant" because this status removes many of the constitutional protections afforded to U.S. citizens. To date, President Bush has declared two American citizens "enemy combatants." Jose Padilla is suspected of planning a "dirty bomb" attack with Al Qaeda and was taken into custody at Chicago's O'Hare airport. Yasser Hamdi was born in the United States but spent most of his life in Saudi Arabia, and was captured on the battlefield in Afghanistan. In December 2003, the Second Circuit Court of Appeals in New York City ruled that President Bush overstepped his authority when he declared Padilla an "enemy combatant." The court ruled that President Bush lacked the power to sidestep the normal legal procedures required when imprisoning a U.S. citizen on American soil.[51] Again, to the extent that this ruling remains in place, the courts are serving to check the executive branch on issues where there are major concerns about the government taking its powers too far.

In June, 2004, the Supreme court went much further in limiting the powers wielded by President Bush by ruling that all enemy combatants—not just American citizens—detained by the U.S. government have a right to contest their detention in a court of law. At issue especially was the group of detainees at a naval base in Guantanamo Bay, Cuba. Bush claimed that because the naval base is in Cuba, it is outside of the jurisdiction of U.S. courts. The Supreme Court, however, ruled that the United States, and not Cuba, had total control over this area and that therefore U.S. laws should apply. Justice Sandra Day O'Connor wrote, ". . . a state of war is not a blank check for the President when it comes to the rights of the Nation's citizens." Justice Antonin Scalia concurred: "The very core of liberty secured by our

Anglo-Saxon system of separated powers has been freedom from indefinite imprisonment at the will of the executive."

Pursuant to this ruling the Bush Administration has set up military panels in front of which detainees may plead their cases, and which may lead to their release. At the same time, civil rights groups have moved to have civilian courts hear the detainees' cases. In either case, to a significant extent the Supreme Court rolled back the power that the Administration claimed to be entitled to in the war against terrorism. The notion that a person, any person—not just an American—can be held by the U.S. government indefinitely without charge and without access to a lawyer or a day in court has been ruled unacceptable. Thus one of the most troubling elements of the PATRIOT Act and its related security measures has been greatly scaled back. Most importantly, by stating that security needs do not give the executive a "blank check" to introduce whatever safety measures it desires, the Supreme Court gave a ringing endorsement to the communitarian idea that we must balance concerns for civil liberties with concerns for security rather than allowing one to trump the other.

Operation TIPS

Operation TIPS (Terrorist Information and Prevention System) initially was meant to be a part of Citizen Corps, the voluntary service the Bush Administration introduced following the president's 2002 State of the Union address and through which Americans can help protect homeland security. Operation TIPS, as it was originally conceived by the White House, was to serve as "a nationwide mechanism for reporting suspicious terrorist activity."[38] Americans would report suspicious activities they encountered to the government by calling a special hotline set up for this purpose.[39] To many people this sounded as if Americans were being asked to snoop on one another and that every mailman, meter reader, and UPS driver might be called upon to peep into one's living room (if not other rooms) and report everything they considered suspicious. If such a program had been implemented, it would have fueled enormous mistrust among Americans. And it would be truly unreasonable because such a program would generate millions of false reports that would over-load authorities, who would fear being blamed for having missed some true nuggets of information in the huge government-generated haystacks of citizens' messages.

Fortunately, Operation TIPS was killed in a little known provision in the Homeland Security Act of 2002 that categorically states that "any and all activities of the Federal Government to implement the proposed component program of the Citizen Corps known as Operation TIPS (Terrorism Information and Prevention System) are hereby prohibited."[40] It should be noted that reference is to reporting suspicious activities, including those that take place in private spaces, especially homes. However, programs are still in place that invite people to report if they see something out of the ordinary in public spaces. For instance, in the spring of 2003, New York City introduced a campaign "If You See Something, Say Something"[41] to convince people riding the subways to stop ignoring one another, a long-established New York tradition, and instead scrutinize those to their left, right, and center.[42] And New York state maintains the tips hotline that it introduced in September 2002.[43] Independent study groups such as the RAND Corporation should examine such programs to determine if they yield significant leads or merely encourage Americans to spy on one another.

Material Support

The new powers include being able to charge someone with a crime for having provided "material support" to terrorists. The Material Support Law was enacted in 1994, extended in 1996[44] in response to the first attack on the World Trade Center,[45] and extended again under the USA PATRIOT Act.[46] It initially appeared that it could take relatively little to hold an American on these grounds because "material support" includes financial assistance, training, expert advice or assistance, and false documentation or identification.[47] For instance, making a donation to the Holy Land Foundation of Richardson, Texas (which claims to support charitable work but actually provides support to Palestinian terrorist groups) could have landed someone in jail whether or not the person was aware of the true purposes of the foundation,[48] until December 2003 when the Ninth Circuit Court of Appeals in San Francisco clarified what "material support" entails. They ruled that individuals or groups cannot be convicted of providing "material support" for terrorist organizations unless the government proves beyond a reasonable doubt that the individuals or groups knew that the organizations were involved in terrorist activity.[49] And more recently, in January 2004, the U.S. District Court in Los Angeles ruled that the phrase "expert advice or assistance" was "impermissibly vague," so much so that the Material Support Law could be interpreted as "unequivocally pure speech and advocacy protected by the First Amendment."[50] To the extent that these rulings remain in place, they do address the most troubling aspect of the "material support" statute.

Overcorrecting the Over-correction?

As there were no new attacks on the homeland in the first two and a half years after September 11, 2001, the public and Congress began swinging in the opposite direction. Demands not to renew portions of the USA PATRIOT Act (some of the measures are due to expire in 2005) increased as did opposition to several other security measures often associated with the PATRIOT Act but not actually part of the bill. As these lines to go press in the summer of 2004, the House of Representatives has voted to extend the PATRIOT Act without revisions.

Earlier, several specific elements of the PATRIOT Act and related security measures were revised, curtailed, dropped—or thus far have been inactive. For instance, Attorney General Ashcroft felt he had to bow to criticism being leveled at section 215 of the Act from organizations such as the American Library Association. This section allows the government—after a court order in cases pertaining to international terrorism—to obtain papers, records, and documents including library records. Ashcroft stated that the measure has not been used since it was enacted.[51] Yet in July, 2004, the House of Representatives, under considerable pressure from the Administration, defeated a proposal to appeal this section of the PATRIOT Act. In the 2004 election cycle President Bush campaigned for its unmodified renewal, without much response from his Democratic challenger, John Kerry. Civil libertarians are particularly strongly opposed to this section of the Act. It is not however immediately obvious—given that the First Amendment allows the publication of designs on how to make dirty bombs, nuclear weapons, and manuals on how to better kill people—that under no circumstances should the government be able to show a jury that a terrorist checked out from a library such materials that he or she then followed to the letter.

The situation is similar with regard to sneak and peek warrants, as laid out in section 213 of the Act. The warrants permit authorities to conduct searches yet delay service of a warrant if it is believed that such action would adversely affect an investigation. If a House appropriations amendment sponsored by Idaho Replication C.L. "Butch" Otter becomes law it will cut off funding for sneak and peek searches. It is not at all clear that this measure is unreasonable. No reasonable person would expect the FBI to leave a business card in the home of a suspected terrorist after it conducted a court-approved search. Especially since the FBI might have to revisit the place or keep it under surveillance.

It is true that almost any of the new security measures may threaten our rights if used wantonly yet they could also be quite acceptable if used under very limited conditions, under the supervision of the courts, Congress, and arguably some special public boards.

Some new measures of accountability are included in the new security laws. The Homeland Security Act contains a provision for an officer whose job it is to protect privacy and another who is to promote civil rights and liberties.[52] In April 2003, the Bush administration appointed Nuala O'Connor Kelly and Daniel W. Sutherland to those respective posts, but it is too soon to tell how much of the needed accountability these officers will be able to deliver.[53] Given the potential for abuse in implementing these last few troubling measures, it would be better if there were a panel of judges, similar to the FISA court, that would regularly review the cases of those Americans charged under these powers. That panel could hold secret hearings to review the cases and release to the public only summary statements and not individualized accounts. For instance, the review panel may find that most, say 80 percent or more, were held appropriately; some, say 15 percent, would require additional information (which in bureaucratic language means "we have doubts about some aspect of their case"); and the remaining few the government would agree to release forthwith due to the urging of the panel.

Measures Yet to Come

So far, these additional safety measures do not include a measure that I consider especially important: improving the reliability of the ways we identify people. Watch lists, airline passenger profiles, student tracking systems, and keeping dossiers on suspects all suffer greatly as long as people can readily obtain false forms of identification (typically driver's licenses) or steal the identity of someone else.

This is no small matter. Driver's licenses are a *de facto* national ID card because, although they are issued by each state, they are honored in all others. Presenting these licenses (or some other such documents, for instance, green cards) are regularly demanded from all those who fly, drive, or enter numerous public buildings and quite a few private ones. Whatever loss of anonymity and privacy is involved, law abiding Americans have already suffered it because they have no reason to carry false IDs. However, as long as terrorists and other criminals can readily obtain fraudulent driver's licenses, many new security measures are fooled. Hence, we need to make driver's licenses meet basic standards of reliability, as has been recommended by the American Association of Motor Vehicle Administrators. Two bills to this effect were introduced in the 107th Congress, one by Representatives James Moran and Tom Davis and the other by Senators Dick Durbin and John McCain; but they garnered little support in Congress.[54]

A subgroup of the Markle Task Force on National Security in the Information Age, which I chaired, examined how to make driver's licenses more reliable by focusing on the process, personnel, and technology involved. The subgroup found that in the short term, there are quite a few measures that may be undertaken to make driver's licenses more reliable. On the process side of things, paper breeder documents should be standardized in order to make it easier to detect counterfeit documents; birth and death records should be digitized and searchable to prevent people from taking the identity of someone who is dead; state motor vehicle departments should verify that the Social Security number the applicant provides actually belongs to him or her; federal legislation should tie the expiration date of a foreign visitor's driver's license or state-issued identification card to the expiration date of his or her visa, as some states have already done; and state driver's licenses and identification cards should meet minimum uniform standards concerning data content and verifiability. Also in the short term, state motor vehicle agencies should provide their employees with ongoing, detailed training about how to spot counterfeit or false documents and they should provide law enforcement personnel with guidelines for how to check the validity of driver's licenses. Aggressive oversight, auditing, and anti-corruption policies can help state motor vehicle agencies prevent fraud and detect it when it occurs in the driver's license issuing process. In the longer term, authorities should study whether biometric and cryptographic technologies can be used to make driver's licenses more reliable; and if so, which technology is appropriate for a driver's license.[55] (For more on this, see Chapter 5.) None of these measures have been undertaken in all states to date.

Conclusion

We should stop pretending that any limitations on our rights (especially in view of the changed world in which we must defend our homeland) amount to an attack on the Constitution. The meaning of our rights has always been subject to interpretation and reinterpretation. At the same time, mindlessly waving aside all claims that we might go overboard for safety's sake is not warranted either. Societies have no precise control mechanisms; they tend to oversteer. Hence, all major corrections in the delicate balance between public safety and civil rights typically require their own corrections. After the September 11 terrorist attack, there were good reasons to rush through legislation expanding government authority, given the fear of more imminent attacks by sleeper cells. Now is the time to revise and fine tune these measures. However, we will be able to see the middle of the road only if both sides stop trying to push the other one over the edge. Extremism in defense of either rights or security is no virtue.

All said and done, several measures that the Bush Administration has launched since the September 11 terrorist attack are, I tried to show, reasonable and necessary. Others may well be necessary but they call for close supervision by Congress to ensure that the government does not yield to the temptations that the given powers pose. Still others must be curbed. Regrettably, there still are some security needs that have not been adequately addressed yet, above all our ability to reliably identify people; in that area, the government needs more, not less, authority.

To reiterate, one may well disagree with my assessment of several of the measures, and new information about the ways that these are used may lead one (including me) to change his or her assessment. However, the approach is of importance: judging each measure rather than lumping them together as if they were all cut from the same cloth.

3
PRIVACY AND SECURITY IN ELECTRONIC COMMUNICATIONS

The general examination of the tension between new security measures and rights here turns much more specific. In this chapter I examine six measures concerning communications surveillance, and among these only the measures relevant to the use of six technologies: cellular phones, the Internet (as a means of communication), high-power encryption, Carnivore, the Key Logger System, and Magic Lantern. I examine the effects of these measures on the use of these technologies and on individual rights and the public interest. The main rights at issue are privacy, anonymity, and due process. The main areas of public interest at issue are public safety and public health, especially prevention of terrorism and response to terrorist attacks once they occur, including bioterrorism.

As I have made clear from the outset, I take it for granted that both individual rights and public safety must be protected, and given that on many occasions advancing one requires some curtailment of the other. The key question is: what is the proper balance between these two cardinal values? The concept of balance is found in the Constitution in the Fourth Amendment. To reiterate, the Fourth Amendment refers to people's right not to be subjected to *un*reasonable search and seizure,[1] hence recognizing a category of searches that are fully compatible with the Constitution: those that are reasonable. Historically, to be considered reasonable, searches have had to serve a compelling public interest, especially public safety or public health.

Much of the debate about the issues at hand in the public arena (by legislatures, opinion makers, and some legal scholars) is conducted by strong advocacy by opposing sides. Thus, one side argues that public safety requires new laws, regulations, and court rulings that would give the government greater surveillance powers, and warns that major calamities will strike if the government is not accorded these powers.[2] Moreover, the advocates of public safety and health claim that the best way to defend liberty is to provide the government with more authority. Dead people are not free.

The other side does not oppose making concessions to public safety, but puts the onus on the government to prove that such concessions are needed and sets the bar very high for such proof, calling for an approach resembling "strict scrutiny."[3] Although, in the debate since the September 11 terrorist attack, the civil libertarians' opening position has been to demand a tighter definition of the conditions under which the new technologies can be applied and closer supervision of the expanded governmental powers, ultimately the classical civil libertarian position is that the government needs no additional powers, and moreover it cannot be trusted to use any of them legitimately.

From the viewpoint of the paradigm used here, each side is speaking for one side of the needed balance rather than seeking to find the point (or better, the zone)[4] at which a carefully crafted balance can be found between protecting the public interest and individual rights.

In line with the communitarian position briefly outlined in the introduction, its starting point—to reiterate—is that there are two valid claims each society faces: the requirements of the public interest (which most obviously encompasses public safety and health, but also encompasses other elements of the common good, such as the protection of the environment) and the requirements of liberty (individual rights included).[5] The "turf" does not belong *a priori* to either claim. It is a gross misconception to argue that public safety measures entail a sacrifice of rights—or vice versa, that respecting individual rights entails sacrifices of the common good. First, in some situations, both can be advanced, such as restoring law and order to a crime-ridden neighborhood or an anarchic country. Second, when the public interest and rights pose conflicting demands, criteria must be developed as to which should take priority, without assuming *a priori* that one automatically trumps the other.[6] Judge Richard Posner put the same basic idea in the following way: "I'll call them the public-safety interest and the liberty interest. Neither, in my view, has priority. They are both important."[7]

The chapter proceeds by first introducing the relevant aspects of three of the six technologies—cellular telephones, the Internet, and encryption—which have expanded people's free choices, and in this sense their liberties, but which have also limited the ability of public authorities to engage in the kind of activities that they are legally entitled to engage in, especially intercepting communications following court approval. I shall refer to these technologies as *liberalizing technologies*. I then examine the arguments in favor of and against changing laws and regulations to enable public authorities to cope with, if not overcome, the hurdles posed by the liberalizing technologies in the post-September 11, 2001 context.

The chapter then turns to the three new technologies that help public authorities—Carnivore, the Key Logger System, and Magic Lantern— which have the opposite profile of the first three: they enhance public safety but they are feared to curb people's rights. I refer to these as security expanding *public protective technologies*. These technologies are then also examined with regard to new laws and regulations and to their effect on the balance between the public interest and individual rights in the post-September 11, 2001 context. The fact that there are new technologies of both kinds further highlights my central thesis that we are not wildly lurching in one direction, but rather that we are working out a balance—albeit a new one—between rights and security.

The chapter section titled "Accountability" calls attention to measures that might help increase public safety while minimizing the threat to individual rights, and focuses on the concept of accountability.

New Liberalizing Technologies

New and Multiple Means of Communication

Before the discussion can proceed, it is essential to note that no attempt is being made here to describe fully or to analyze the technologies at issue, but merely to point to features of them that are relevant to the issues at hand. The year 1980 is used as a baseline. At the time, the most convenient, and by far the most commonly used, way to communicate instantaneously with a person at a different location was through a wired telephone. Cellular phones existed but they were not yet commercially viable nor were they available in models lightweight enough to put in a pocket.[8] Fax machines had not yet come into wide use.[9] Telegraphs required, as a rule, going to a post office or Western Union location. Most people had one phone line, even if they had more than one extension. The Internet was still the ARPANET, a government sponsored network linking mainly universities and research centers.[10] In 1980 all necessary communications surveillance could be carried out easily by attaching simple devices to a suspect's one landline telephone.[11]

In the following two decades, many millions of people acquired several alternative modes of convenient, instantaneous communication, most significantly cellular telephones and e-mail. By July 2000, there were over 100 million cell phone subscribers in the United States.[12] E-mail and Internet usage are similarly pervasive. Nielsen/Net Rating estimated that in July of 2001, 165.2 million people in the United States had home Internet access.[13]

These technological developments greatly limited the ability of public authorities to conduct communications surveillance using traditional methods under old laws (those in effect before the passage of the USA PATRIOT Act, the provisions of which will be discussed later in this chapter). Attempts were made to apply old laws to new technologies but they did not fit well. To proceed, it must be noted that there are two types of communications surveillance: public authorities get "pen register" and "trap and trace" orders to obtain only the numbers dialed to or from a specific telephone,[14] or they get full intercept orders to listen to the content of a telephone call.[15] Because the information involved in the first type is less sensitive, these orders are much easier to get than the latter.[16] The terms "pen register" and "trap and trace" refer to the devices originally used to carry out the trace orders.[17] Although the technologies they refer to have been replaced, these terms are still commonly used. I will use the term "pen/trap" to designate the type of communications surveillance that involves gathering only the numbers dialed to and from a telephone, or their e-mail equivalent. The term "full intercept" will refer to wiretaps and other means of intercepting the full content of a communication. The term "communications surveillance" will include both pen/trap and full intercept orders.

The law governing full intercepts, contained in Title III of the Omnibus Crime Control and Safe Streets Act of 1969,[18] required that court orders for intercepts specify the location of the communications device to be tapped and establish probable cause that evidence of criminal conduct could be collected by tapping that particular device. Hence, under this law, if a suspect shifted from one phone to another or used multiple phones, the government could not legally tap phones other than the one originally specified without obtaining a separate court order for each.[19] Once criminals were able to obtain multiple cell phones and to "dispose of them as used tissues,"[20] investigations were greatly hindered by the lengthy process of obtaining numerous full intercept authorizations from the courts.[21]

The rise of Internet-based communications further limited the ability of public authorities to conduct communications surveillance under the old laws. Because Title III did not originally apply to electronic communications, e-mail was often treated as analogous to an older form of communication in the courts.[22] Because e-mails used to largely travel over phone lines, officials extended laws governing interception or traces for telephones to govern interception and traces of e-mails as well.[23] However, the language of the old legislation governing pen/trap orders was not clearly applicable to e-mail communications.[24] Although police used pen/trap orders to trace e-mail messages, there was a possibility that a court would rule that e-mail did not fall under pen/trap orders if this was ever challenged in court.[25]

Furthermore, deregulation of the telecommunications industry created additional complications in carrying out pen/trap orders. When the old legislation went into effect, a unified phone network made it easy to identify the source of a call.[26] But e-mail can pass through multiple service providers in different locations throughout the nation on its way from sender to recipient. This means that a service provider might only be able to inform public authorities that a message came from another service provider. In this case, public authorities would have to obtain a new court order from the jurisdiction of that provider to find out where the message came from.[27] Thus, until recently, if a message went through four providers, four court orders in four different jurisdictions would be needed to find out the origin of that message.

As with pen/trap orders, the original laws governing full intercept orders did not initially apply to e-mail. However, the Electronic Communications Privacy Act of 1986[28] extended the full intercept laws to apply to electronic communications.[29] E-mail messages differ from phone conversations in important ways that have made the old laws, at best, an imperfect fit.[30] E-mails do not travel over phone lines in discrete units that can just be plucked out. They are broken up into digital packets and they travel through the Internet using different routes, mixed together with the packets of the messages of other users.[31] This creates a challenge for law enforcement agents attempting to intercept or trace the e-mail of just one user without violating the privacy of other users.[32]

Problems also occurred when agents received the same search warrants to obtain saved e-mail that they would use in any other physical search.[33] Under old laws, a warrant must be obtained from a judge in the jurisdiction where the search will take place.[34] E-mail, however, is not always stored on a personal computer but often is stored remotely on the servers of Internet service providers (ISPs). This means that if a suspect, say, in New Jersey had e-mail stored on a server located in, say, Silicon Valley, an agent would have to travel across the country to get a warrant to seize the e-mail.[35]

In short, the introduction of both cellular phones and e-mail created new challenges to the ability of public authorities to conduct communications intercepts, even if they were fully authorized by a court—intercepts that had been an important tool of law enforcement. Another technological development has made communications intercepts much more difficult still. Before it is introduced, a brief digression. There is a tendency in parts of the literature on privacy to argue that new technological developments have gravely undermined privacy, if not killed it altogether.[36] In effect, however, the situation in this area is akin to an arms race: as new means of attack are developed, so are new means of defense, although in any given period one side or the other may be the leading beneficiary of new technological developments.

To return to our subject, a major technological development that greatly enhances privacy—and potentially sets back the ability of public authorities to intercept communications—is high-power encryption.[37] Although codes have existed for thousands of years,[38] only over the last few have programmers developed encryption systems that use codes 128 bits or longer, which are said to be impossible to crack, even by the National Security Agency (NSA).[39] Moreover, these programs are readily available to private parties at low costs. Stewart Baker, former general counsel for the NSA, said that "encryption is virtually unbreakable by police today, with programs that can be bought for $15."[40] Indeed, these programs are increasingly being routinely built into computers."[41] *This means that the privacy of encrypted messages is much higher than that of any messages historically sent by mail, phone, messenger, carrier pigeon, or other means.* (The same encryption also allows the storing of information in one's computer—personal or corporate— that is much better protected than it ever was under lock and key, or even in safes.)[42]

High-power encryption has caused a major setback for law enforcement.[43] Even when granted a court order, public authorities simply seem unable to implement it.[44]

The consequence of this development has been different from others created by new technologies. In contrast with the situation concerning the multiplication of means of expeditious communication, in which the main factor that constrained public authorities was the obsolescence of laws, in the case of high power encryption, the new technology imposes a barrier all its own. In the other instance, a change of law was sufficient to enable law enforcement to deal with the new challenges posed by the new technologies. Here, the horse was out of the barn by September 11, 2001. It seems impossible to break high-power encryption, whatever the courts may authorize.

Legal Responses

All in all, these technological developments have provided law abiding citizens as well as criminals, including terrorists, greater freedom to do as they choose, and in this sense they are "liberalizing." At the same time, they have significantly hampered the ability of public authorities to conduct investigations. Some cyberspace enthusiasts welcomed these developments, hoping that cyberspace would be a self regulating, government-free space.[45] In contrast, public authorities clamored for changing the laws to enable them to act in the new "territory" as they do in the world of old fashioned, landline telephones.[46] Their pressures led to some modifications in the law before the 2001 attack on America, although the most relevant changes in the law have occurred since then. Both the pre- and post-September 11, 2001, changes to expand the relevant intercept powers of the authorities are next examined jointly.

Roving Intercepts The Electronic Communications Privacy Act of 1986 (ECPA) attempted to update the laws governing communications intercepts to be able to deal with the limitations put on them by the technological developments already discussed by allowing for what are known as "roving wiretaps" in criminal investigations.[47] Roving wiretaps are full intercept orders that apply to a *particular person*, rather than to a *specific communications device*. They allow law enforcement to obtain a court order to intercept that person's communications, without specifying in advance which facilities will be tapped, allowing officers to intercept communications from any phone or computer that the person uses.[48]

The process for obtaining a roving intercept order is more rigorous than that for obtaining the old kind of phone specific order. The Attorney General's office must approve the application before it is even brought before a judge.[49] Originally, the applicant had to show that the suspect named in the application was changing phones or modems frequently with the *purpose* of thwarting interception,[50] but the Intelligence Authorization Act for Fiscal Year 1999 made it easier to obtain a roving intercept order by replacing the requirement to show "purpose to thwart" with the requirement to show that the suspect is changing phones or modems frequently, and that this practice "could have the effect of thwarting" the investigation.[51] Although roving intercepts have not yet been tested in the Supreme Court, several federal courts have found them constitutional.[52]

Prior to the September 11 terrorist attack, the FBI could not gain authorization for using roving intercepts in gathering foreign intelligence or in investigations of terrorism. The USA PATRIOT Act allows for such roving intercept orders to be granted under the Federal Intelligence Surveillance Act (FISA).[53] FISA was passed in 1978 and provides the guidelines under which the executive branch—not only the president but also the Department of Justice—can obtain authorization to conduct surveillance for foreign intelligence purposes.[54] Agents who wish to conduct surveillance under FISA submit an application first to the Attorney General's office, which must approve all requests (as with roving intercepts under ECPA). If the Attorney General's Office finds the application valid, it will be taken to one of seven federally appointed judges, who together make up the Federal Intelligence and Security Court (FISC), for approval. The FISC allows no spectators, keeps most proceedings secret, and hears only the government side of a case.[55]

Initially, FISA was limited to investigations for which foreign intelligence was the sole purpose. The USA PATRIOT Act modifies FISA so that foreign intelligence need be only a "significant purpose" of an investigation.[56] This change effectively allows FISA to be used as part of "multi-faceted responses to terrorism, which involves foreign intelligence and criminal investigations."[57] Because FISA was originally designed for use in gathering foreign intelligence, communications surveillance conducted under FISA differs from that conducted under Title III criminal investigations in several other ways. Under normal Title III intercepts, anyone whose communications have been intercepted has to be notified after the fact that this happened. Under FISA, people do not have to be notified unless evidence obtained through the interception is to be used against them in court.[58] When lawyers use FISA evidence in court, it is difficult for the defendant to challenge it because he or she cannot see the information that agents relied on in making the application for surveillance—this is secret for national security reasons.[59]

E-mail Surveillance The USA PATRIOT Act includes provisions that make it easier for public authorities to trace or seize e-mail messages. It explicitly allows pen/trap orders for computer communications (as already discussed, previous orders had to rely on stretched interpretations of the statutes governing pen/trap for telephones).[60] Traces on telephone lines can usually be fulfilled by the local phone company that issued the line. Tracing e-mail messages, which travel through a variety of routes and may go through multiple carriers, often requires access at different points across the country.[61] As previously explained, following the phone model requires gaining warrants in several locations in order to trace one e-mail message. The USA PATRIOT Act establishes what are *de facto* nationwide pen/trap orders,[62] allowing one court order to be used on all the carriers through which messages from an individual pass. When a law enforcement agent discovers that an e-mail message was forwarded to (or from) any carrier, he can serve the original court order to this carrier without getting an additional order from the court in whose jurisdiction the carrier is located. Moreover, because agents cannot know in advance which carriers will be involved, the court order needs to specify only the initial facility at which the pen/trap order will be carried out.

The USA PATRIOT Act also allows a judge in the district with jurisdiction over the crime under investigation to grant search warrants to seize electronic communications stored outside that judge's jurisdiction.[63] This means that an agent can obtain a warrant from a judge in the jurisdiction where the investigation is taking place to seize e-mail stored by an ISP physically located in another jurisdiction.[64]

Dealing with Encryption Previous administrations tried to have "back doors" built into encryption software that would enable public authorities, when needed, to decrypt reportedly unbreakable codes.[65] They also attempted to get legislation passed that would require users to deposit a copy of their key with third parties (referred to as "escrow") or public authorities, who would not be able to look at or use the key unless authorized to do so as part of an investigation.[66] A combination of civil liberties groups and high-tech corporations successfully fought off both of these attempts.[67] No attempts to deal with this matter were included in the USA PATRIOT Act. I will discuss law enforcement tools designed to cope with encryption in my discussion of the public protective technologies.

Evaluating the Changes in the Law The adaptations of the laws governing communications surveillance (which includes both pen/trap and full intercept orders) and seizures of stored communications have been subject to both general and detailed debates by the adversarial advocates already mentioned. On the general level, these adaptations were lumped together with numerous other matters, including indefinite detention of aliens,[68] allowing the government to listen in on attorney-client conversations,[69] and military tribunals.[70] The nature of the debate on this level is illustrated by statements such as Senator Leahy's that some of the measures are "shredding the Constitution"[71] and Morton Halperin's reference to the legislation as "Striking Terror at Civil Liberty."[72] On the other side, Senator Hatch dismissed such misgivings as "hysterical concerns" and said the American people do not want to see Congress "quibble about whether we should provide more rights than the Constitution requires to the criminals and terrorists who are devoted to killing our people."[73]

There has been some debate in the courts and among legal scholars as to how to apply the Fourth Amendment to the new technologies, as well as to the constitutionality of the new legislation governing these technologies. Before 1967, the Supreme Court interpreted the Fourth Amendment in a literal way, as applying only to *physical* searches. In the 1928 case of *Olmstead v. United States,* the Court took a strict interpretation of the Fourth Amendment and ruled that telephone wiretaps did not constitute a search unless public authorities entered a home to install the device and that therefore the Fourth Amendment did not apply to them.[74] The justices wrote in their decision that a person is not protected under the Fourth Amendment unless "there has been an official search and seizure of his person, or such a seizure of his papers or his tangible effects, or an actual physical invasion of his house."[75]

In 1967 the Court replaced this interpretation of the Fourth Amendment with the view that it "protects people, not places."[76] In *Katz v. United States,* the Court established a new guideline for determining what falls under the protection of the Fourth Amendment, which is still in use today—that of a reasonable expectation of privacy.[77] Justice Harlan, in his concurring opinion, set out a two-part test for determining if Fourth Amendment protection applies: the individual must have shown an expectation of privacy, and society must recognize that expectation as reasonable.[78]

Legal scholars have criticized reasonable expectation as the cornerstone of the legal privacy doctrine,[79] but the doctrine is generally still used as a guiding principle. As new technologies emerge, however, the question of what constitutes a reasonable expectation of privacy has to be reexamined in this new context. In the 1996 case of *United States v. Maxwell*, the courts determined that there was a reasonable expectation of privacy for e-mail stored on a server,[80] giving this e-mail, in essence, the same protections given to paper documents stored in an office. In the case of *United States v. Charbonneau*, however, the courts determined that the extent to which one can expect privacy in e-mail communications depends on the context of the situation.[81]

Lt. Col. Joginder Dhillon and Lt. Col. Robert Smith argue that because e-mail messages reside on numerous servers between the sending and receiving server, and because on many networks duplicate copies of all e-mails are sent to the system administrator, there may not be a reasonable expectation of privacy for e-mail.[82] This interpretation is backed up by the Supreme Court case *Smith v. Maryland*, in which the Court found that there is no reasonable expectation of privacy for the telephone numbers one dials because those numbers must be conveyed to the phone company.[83] Dhillon and Smith conclude that, at the very least, *Smith v. Maryland* should mean that recording the addressing information of e-mail does not require a full intercept order.[84]

There is some question as to whether or not roving intercepts are in compliance with the Fourth Amendment's *particularity* requirement. The requirement that intercept orders specify the place of the intercept comes from the Fourth Amendment, which states that "no warrants shall issue, but upon probable cause, supported by oath or affirmation, and particularly describing the place to be searched, and the persons or things to be seized."[85] Because roving intercepts do not name the location to be tapped, there is some question as to whether or not they are constitutional under the Fourth Amendment.

The argument in favor of their constitutionality is that the particularity of the *person* to be tapped is substituted for the particularity of the *place* to be tapped. In the case of *United States v. Petti*, the Ninth Circuit Court of Appeals upheld the use of roving intercepts, arguing that the purpose of the particularity requirement was to prevent general searches.[86] So long as a warrant or court order provides "sufficient particularity to enable the executing officer to locate and identify the premises with reasonable effort" and there is no "reasonable probability that another premise might be mistakenly searched," it is in compliance with the Fourth Amendment.[87] A court order to tap all phones that a specific person uses *does* describe particular places, but in an unconventional way. Public authorities cannot use the order to tap any location they wish, but only a set of specific locations that they can show are used by a specific person.[88]

Not everyone agrees that this substitution of particularity of person for particularity of place is sufficient to satisfy the Fourth Amendment. Tracey Maclin cites the Supreme Court case of *Steagald v. United States* in which the Court concluded that an arrest warrant that specifies a person cannot be used to search private places not named in the warrant in pursuit of that person.[89] She interprets this decision to mean that the Court found warrants to be flawed that specify only the target of the search, but leave police to determine which particular locations to search. Maclin argues that although roving intercepts are issued for one person, once public authorities decide to "tap" a telephone or computer, everyone using that telephone or computer will be subject to surveillance, so there is no true particularity of person maintained.[90]

In his analysis of the issue, Clifford Fishman finds that although relevant Fourth Amendment case law does not give conclusive support either for or against roving intercepts, there are strong arguments in favor of their constitutionality. He holds that roving intercept orders "describe the 'place' to be searched in a somewhat untraditional, but still sufficiently particular way" and argues that "if the Fourth Amendment is flexible enough to protect privacy against technological developments far beyond the contemplation of the founding fathers, then it must also be flexible enough to permit investigators to preserve the basic mandate of the amendment's particularity requirement in a novel way."[91]

Numerous additional questions arise regarding the difference in applying the new laws, as well as the old ones, to noncitizens versus citizens, to terrorists versus criminals, and to international versus domestic terrorists. These are huge issues that concern the extent to which the Constitution applies to noncitizens, in the United States and elsewhere, and what rights noncitizens have. These issues raise potential problems, such as how to define terrorism and whether that definition should extend to citizens, as well as the danger that a loose definition might allow ordinary criminals to be encompassed by terrorism laws. These issues go well beyond communications technology and the laws related to it.

Proponents of roving intercepts argue that without them authorities will see a "whole operation frustrated because a terrorist throws away a telephone and picks up another phone and then moves on."[92] Critics argue that the new law will ensnarl many innocent people unrelated to investigations. Civil libertarians like Nadine Strossen argue that the new law, as it relates to roving intercepts, "goes far beyond" facilitating investigations based on individual suspicion. She uses the example of a suspected terrorist who sends an e-mail from a public library computer terminal. If the computer is tapped, any of the other users, who have no connection to the suspect, will also have their communications intercepted.[93] The same critics contend that issuing nationwide warrants just allows law enforcement agents to "shop for friendly judges."[94] Senator Hatch counters that these provisions and others merely fix parts of the criminal code that formerly treated terrorists "with kid gloves."[95]

It is worth noting that although the ACLU does not exempt the laws at issue from its heavy criticism of the new measures, when explicitly asked whether it would at least recognize that allowing public authorities to tap all phones used by the same person was eminently reasonable, it hinted that it is somewhat less troubled by the changes in the laws under discussion here than by many of the other measures.[96] Alan Dershowitz, a longtime defender of civil liberties, even went so far as to concede that roving intercepts are "a very good idea."[97]

The ACLU criticizes changes in FISA, which it charges allow authorities to "bypass normal criminal procedures that protect privacy and take checks and balances out of the law."[98] Civil libertarians worry about the USA PATRIOT Act's extension of the reach of FISA, which provides fewer protections than are provided for criminal cases, as the discussion above regarding full intercepts under FISA illustrates. (Civil libertarians' concerns about pen/trap orders for e-mail are discussed in the section on protective technologies.)

* * *

I shall defer my own assessment of the legitimacy of the new legal adaptations to the liberalizing technologies, and of their effects on the balance between individual rights and public safety and health, until I review the next three technologies and the laws concerning them. For now it might serve to remind that I am not dealing with the general legitimacy of FISA or the USA PATRIOT Act, but with some elements of these laws, specifically those that concern communications surveillance. This is significant to keep in mind because conclusions about other elements—military tribunals and indefinite detention of suspects, for instance—may be different than those about the surveillance laws at issue.

Public Protective Technologies

The discussion now turns to three technologies that have the opposite profile of those explored so far: they enhance the capabilities of public authorities and they raise fears that they will curtail individual rights.

Carnivore

Carnivore, a computer program unveiled by the FBI in July 2000, is used to trace and seize Internet communications. To capture a suspect's messages or trace messages sent to and from his account, public authorities must sort through a stream of many millions of messages, including those of many other users as well as those of the suspect. Some ISPs have the capability of doing this sorting themselves and will simply pass the appropriate information on to agents after a warrant or court order is presented. If an ISP is not capable of doing this kind of sorting, the FBI uses Carnivore to do it.[99]

Carnivore runs as an application program on an operating system and works by screening e-mails and sorting them based on a "filter," which tells the program which information to capture and which to merely let pass by. The filter can be set to sort out messages from a specific computer or e-mail address, or it can scan various packets to find a specific text string.[100] Carnivore can be set to operate in two different modes: "pen" and "full." In pen mode it will capture only the addressing information (which includes the e-mail addresses of the sender and recipient, as well as the subject line) while in full mode it will capture the entire content of a message.[101] Carnivore is designed to copy and store only information caught by the filter, thus keeping agents from looking at any addressing information or e-mail content not covered in the court order.[102]

Carnivore's pen mode is of value to public authorities even if the messages themselves cannot be read, such as in the growing number of cases in which high-power encryption is used, because the government benefits from an analysis of the addresses. For instance, it can use pen/trap orders to trace to whom a group of suspects addresses their e-mail. When used in this capacity, it would make more sense to call Carnivore (which hardly devours the messages, despite its name) a communications traffic analyzer.

As of the fall of 2000, the FBI said that it had used Carnivore "approximately 25 times in the last two years."[103] The Carnivore program is stored in an FBI laboratory and only brought out when needed to fulfill a specific court order. After the court order has expired, officials return the program to the laboratory.[104]

The Key Logger System and Magic Lantern

Despite the introduction of Carnivore, the government seems to be greatly hobbled by its inability to decrypt a rapidly growing proportion of all messages. To overcome this limitation, the FBI is introducing two new technologies to obtain a suspect's password. A password can enter or exit the encryption/decryption process in four ways: going over a modem, retrieval from storage, entry into a keyboard, or a process working within the computer itself.[105] The Key Logger System (KLS), developed by the FBI, has several components that work together to obtain someone's password.[106]

Once agents discover that information they have seized through a warranted search or intercepted with a proper court order is encrypted, they can obtain another warrant to install and retrieve the KLS.[107] In the case of Nicodemo Scarfo, who was suspected of racketeering, agents had to show both probable cause that Scarfo was involved in crime and probable cause that important information was installed on his computer in encrypted form. As in any warrant, the FBI had to specify the exact location of the computer on which the KLS would be installed.[108]

Once installed, the KLS uses a "keystroke capture" device to record keystrokes as they are entered into a computer. It is not capable of searching or recording fixed data stored on the computer, or of intercepting electronic communications sent to and from the computer (which would require an intercept order, which is more difficult to get than a warrant). In order not to intercept inadvertently the content of communications, the KLS is designed so that it is unable to record keystrokes while a computer's modem is in operation.[109]

Because the KLS must be installed manually and covertly on a suspect's computer, which involves breaking and entering, it is arguably more invasive than "backdoors" and key escrow (which, as previously discussed, are not available, due mainly to opposition by civil libertarians and high-tech business interests).[110] Those who are shocked by this technology should consider the effects of high-power encryption. As the *Boston Globe's* technology reporter commented, "techno-libertarians rightly howled when the feds tried to bar access to encryption software; now we must live with the consequences. The bad guys have encryption. The good guys must have counter-encryption tools."[111]

The FBI has revealed that it has been developing a less invasive technology. In November 2001, the FBI admitted that it had developed, but not yet implemented, a remote-control approach called Magic Lantern that allows the FBI to put software on a computer that will record keystrokes typed without installing any physical device.[112] Like the KLS, Magic Lantern does not by itself decrypt e-mail but it can obtain the suspect's password. The details of how it does this have not been released.[113] It is said to install itself on the suspect's computer in a way similar to a Trojan horse computer virus. It disguises itself as ordinary, harmless code, then inserts itself onto a computer. For example, the FBI will have a box pop up when someone connects to the Internet reading something like "Click here to win." When the user clicks on the box, the virus will enter the computer.[114]

Evaluating the New Technologies

Just as laws were put in place both before and after the September 11 terrorist attack to limit the concerns that new liberalizing technologies posed for public safety, some have also introduced measures that limit the use of new protective technologies and address the concerns they pose for individual rights. Most of the limitations on the use of Carnivore and the KLS were put in place as these technologies developed and before they were used, although there have also been "additions" to the checks placed on them. The shift from the KLS to Magic Lantern can be considered an improvement from a rights viewpoint because it will not require covert breaking and entering by a law enforcement agent to install it on a suspect's office or home computer.

Nevertheless, both Carnivore and the KLS have raised concerns on the part of privacy advocates and civil liberties groups. Critics are skeptical that the programs operate the way that the FBI claims they do and they are troubled by the degree of secrecy the FBI maintains regarding how the programs work.

Groups like the Electronic Privacy Information Center (EPIC) and the Center for Democracy and Technology (CDT) have multiple arguments for why Carnivore should not be used at all. They argue that because, for e-mail, it is much harder to separate addressing information from content than for a phone call, Carnivore will not allow the FBI to do a pen/trap without seizing more information than authorized.[115] Privacy advocates also worry that Carnivore will scan through "tens of millions of e-mails and other communications from innocent Internet users as well as the targeted suspect,"[116] thus violating the Fourth Amendment.[117] The ACLU compares a Carnivore search to the FBI sending agents into a post office to "rip open each and every mail bag and search for one person's letters" and to "tapping the entire phone exchange system, listening to all the conversations, and then keeping only the ones that are incriminating, instead of tapping a single phone line."[118] A *USA Today* editorial stated that "once it's in place, Carnivore acts as an unrestrained Internet wiretap, snooping through every Internet communication that comes within its reach."[119]

Officials at the FBI respond that Carnivore, when used properly, will pull out only the appropriate e-mails, and that its use is subject to strict internal review and requires the cooperation of technical specialists and ISP personnel, thus limiting the opportunities an unscrupulous agent might have to abuse it. In Donald Kerr's words, the FBI does not have "the right or the ability to just go fishing."[120]

A review of Carnivore conducted by the Illinois Institute of Technology concluded that although it does not completely eliminate the risk of capturing unauthorized information, Carnivore is better than any existing alternatives and should continue to be used.[121] However, the panel also determined that the FBI's internal audit process is insufficient to protect against improper use.[122] Specifically, the operator implementing a Carnivore search selects either pen or full mode by clicking one box on a computer screen;[123] and because the program does not keep track of what kind of search has been run,[124] it is difficult to determine if an operator has used the program only as specified in the court order. The head of the Illinois panel commented: "Even if you conclude that the software is flawless and it will do exactly what you set it to do and nothing more, you still have to make sure that the legal, human and organizational controls are adequate."[125] I turn to this matter below, when discussing accountability.

There is a tendency to attribute to computers human traits and talk or write about them as if they "sniff" and "snoop," violate privacy, and so on. One day, computers may achieve such human capabilities; but for now, a computer does not ogle, snicker at, or get aroused by a picture of a nude person because it does not "see"; its "mind" processes merely ones and zeros. Thus, if millions of messages flow through a computer running Carnivore, none of them is "read" *unless* it is caught by the filter and passed on to a human observer.[126] Computers do not "read" or "scan" messages any more than phones "listen" to messages left in their voice mail boxes. The issue is what humans do—not machines. True, if new technological capabilities did not exist or their use were fully banned— an old Luddite argument[127]—the problem would not arise in the first place. However, as long as new technologies are available to criminal elements, it is hard to argue in favor of privileging them and blocking the government from using countermeasures under the proper conditions.

The legality of the KLS was tested in the case of Nicodemo Scarfo, in which the FBI used the KLS to decrypt records implicating Scarfo in racketeering. Scarfo's defense argued that the key logger records keystrokes typed in electronic communications and sent over a modem, and should therefore have required a full intercept order, rather than an easier to obtain search warrant. Although the FBI says that the KLS cannot record while a modem is in operation, thus protecting against the capture of electronic communications, Scarfo and the privacy advocates interested in the case were skeptical. During the trial, lawyers showed Scarfo a hard copy of all the keystrokes intercepted, but was unable to pick out anything that he recognized as being part of an electronic communication.[128]

Scarfo also argued that the warrant used to install the KLS violated the particularity requirement of the Fourth Amendment and therefore constituted a general search because it did not describe specifically what could be searched and seized.[129] The warrant in the case authorized FBI agents to "install and leave behind software, firmware, and/or hardware equipment which will monitor the inputted data entered on Nicodemo S. Scarfo's computer in the TARGET LOCATION," which was specified in great detail. The same warrant authorized the surreptitious breaking and entry into the target location to install and retrieve the KLS and also authorized the FBI to seize business records "in whatever form they are kept."[130] David Sobel of EPIC said that because the warrant was issued to get one password, but the KLS recorded every keystroke typed, it was comparable to if a police officer got "a warrant to seize one book in your house, but was also allowed to haul out everything that's in there."[131] Although it is true that in the Scarfo case agents had to look through all keystrokes entered after the installation of the KLS in order to pick out the string that was his password, the FBI argues that this is similar to any search. If public authorities have a warrant to get someone's account book from their office, they may have to look through many drawers and shelves before finding it.[132] In December 2001, the judge in the Scarfo case ruled that the use of the KLS to obtain his password was legal and constituted neither a general search nor a form of surveillance.[133] This seems eminently reasonable—as long as such a search is based on a warrant or some other form of judicial review. It points, however, to the issue next explored: what is a sufficient level of supervision for any and all police actions, including for the FBI?

Accountability

The Second Balance

There is need for balance between individual rights and public safety and health, rather than one or the other predominating. Thus, when the state or government tilts too far toward safety or rights, such tilts are best corrected. The question hence arises as to what effects the new technologies have on this balance. There can be little doubt that (a) the liberalizing technologies have greatly hindered the work of public authorities in the area of communications surveillance; however (b) new protective technologies to some extent overcome these difficulties. The same might be said about (c) new legislation that did adapt the old applicable laws to the new technologies. Finally (d): the 2001 attack on America changed what I call the "zone of balance" by posing a new, credible threat to public safety and health. This still leaves open the question of whether the new measures, whether technological or legal, provide for much-needed enhanced public safety or excessively intrude into individual rights.

This, in turn, raises the question of how generally to determine whether or not the state is in the zone of balance. This is an issue with which the courts have struggled for generations; it would take volumes to begin to do it justice.[134] I have concluded elsewhere that the course of a nation's laws should not be corrected unless there is a compelling reason (a concept akin to "clear and present danger," although not necessarily one that meets this criterion technically); unless the matter cannot be addressed by nonlegal, voluntary means; and unless one can make the intrusion small and the gain (either in safety or in rights) considerable. Further specification draws on what a reasonable person would find sensible, taking into account that the Constitution is a living document whose interpretation has been adjusted through the ages.

These criteria can be applied to the issues discussed here. For example, in the post-September 11, 2001, context, it is clear that the government should have greater powers to decrypt e-mail because terrorism does pose a major threat; voluntary means to fight encrypted terrorist messages have not sufficed on the face of it; and enabling and allowing the government to decrypt e-mail messages is not more intrusive than tapping a phone and can be allowed under similar conditions. The authority to use roving wiretaps may pass the same test. (To reiterate, other public safety measures recently introduced that do not concern communications surveillance, such as requiring protesters to remove their disguises, are not discussed here and may very well not meet the criteria listed.)[135]

Yet, to determine fully whether or not a given new measure that enhances the powers of public authorities is called for, I suggest that a second form of balancing needs to be considered that, arguably, in the matters at hand, may turn out to be decisive compared to the first form already discussed. It concerns not whether the government should be accorded new powers, but how closely it is held accountable regarding the ways it uses these powers. From this viewpoint, the key issue is not if certain powers—for example, the ability to decrypt e-mail—should or should not be available to public authorities, but whether or not these powers are used legitimately and whether mechanisms are in place to ensure such usage.[136]

Although these two forms of balance have some similarities and points of overlap, they are quite distinct. Thus, to argue, as cyber-libertarians do, that the government should not be allowed to decrypt encoded messages or demand from an ISP the addressing information for e-mail sent to and from a suspect's account, and so on, is different from agreeing that such powers are justified so long as they are properly circumscribed and their use is duly supervised.

The balance sought here is not between the public interest and rights, but between the supervised and the supervisors. Deficient accountability opens the door to government abuses of power; excessively tight controls make for agents who are reluctant to act.

Thus, as described in the introduction to this book, a case can be made that in the decades preceding the Church Commission, under most of Hoover's reign, the FBI was insufficiently accountable; and that after the Commission's rules were institutionalized, the FBI was excessively limited prior to the September 11 terrorist attack in what it was allowed to do in the area of communications surveillance. Agents, fearing reprimands and damage to their careers, were often too reluctant to act.

To elaborate a bit, it seems difficult to sustain the argument that the government should be unable to decrypt any messages or be unable to gain the authority to do so. After the first bombing of the World Trade Center in 1993, one of its principal masterminds used encryption to protect files on his laptop computer as he plotted to blow up commercial airlines.[137] (Encrypted files were found on a computer used by Osama bin Laden's lieutenants in the Afghan capital.[138]) Few would argue that public authorities should be unable to decrypt such files, even, say, after obtaining a warrant based on probable cause that the files included important information.

The issue hence becomes which limits will be set and what messages can be decrypted, who will verify that these limits are observed, and by what means. Similarly, regarding roving intercepts, the issue is not whether the government should have to get a warrant for each instrument of communication that the same suspect uses, but by what means it will be ensured that the government does not collect information about other people who use the same instruments of communication or the same computer terminal. The key issue is not whether communications in cyberspace should be exempted from the same type of public scrutiny to which mail and phone calls have historically been subject, as cyber-idealists had hoped,[139] but whether there are proper controls in place to protect against abuse.

The next step in assessing whether or not the American polity, in matters concerning communications surveillance, is currently excessively attentive to public safety or not willing to take needed measures out of excessive concern for rights. This will be based on determining to what extent accountability has been built into the new powers granted to the government in response to the new technologies at hand and in reaction to the September 11 terrorist attack.

Layers of Accountability: Limitations Built into the Law

Limitations on the use of new powers are written into the laws governing them and limitations on protective technologies are often built into the technologies themselves. Roving intercepts, and indeed any intercepts, are not granted without limits. Title III lays out a requirement for "minimization," stated at follows: "Every order and extension thereof shall contain a provision that the authorization to intercept shall be executed as soon as practicable, shall be conducted in such a way as to minimize the interception under this chapter, and must terminate upon attainment of the authorized objective, or in any event in thirty days."[140]

Such built-in guidelines are intended to limit the ability of public authorities to gather and use information not directly related to their investigations.[141] Practically, this means that agents are not allowed to record conversations that are unrelated to the subject of the investigation and should stop listening when irrelevant matters are being discussed. If agents are unsure if a seemingly innocent conversation might touch on a relevant subject at some point, agents are to conduct "spot monitoring," in which they tune in every few minutes to check, but only begin to record when appropriate.[142]

In *Scott v. United States*,[143] the Supreme Court found that an agent's implementation of such guidelines must be evaluated under a "standard of objective reasonableness," so that if circumstances make minimization difficult, failure by an agent to attempt it does not constitute a violation of the law.[144] In addition, if investigators have reason to suspect a conspiracy involving a large number of people, they are justified in recording and listening to all conversations until they are certain who is innocent and who is not.[145] Many critics point out that under any circumstances, minimization is voluntary and we must rely on our trust in law enforcement officers to do it properly, highlighting the importance of further layers of accountability, such as the exclusionary rule.[146]

Although telephone wiretaps rely on human judgment in implementing minimization, new public protective technologies, if properly used, carry out much of the minimization function automatically. Carnivore's filters, if set properly, act as a built-in minimization process, intercepting only what is appropriate. Although it might be capable of collecting all content that passes through it, in compliance with court orders it should be set to capture only data sent to and from a specific user.[147] As mentioned, data that does not fit the filter settings just passes through without being saved by Carnivore, and is therefore not seen by public authorities.[148]

Supervision within Executive Agencies

Numerous accountability mechanisms are built into the executive agencies of the government. Of course, FBI field agents are subject to numerous guidelines and supervisors whose jobs include ensuring that these guidelines are abided by. They, in turn, report to still higher ranking supervisors. Moreover, when agents cross the line, internal reviews take place. In addition, the Attorney General's Office to some extent supervises what the FBI does. Although some may say that this is like asking the fox to guard the henhouse, the following lines suggest that such supervision is not meaningless, although it is far from sufficient in itself.

For instance, as already mentioned, requests by the FBI to conduct communications surveillance under FISA must be approved by the Attorney General's Office before they are submitted to the FISC. In some cases, court orders or warrant requests never get past internal FBI approval procedures. For example, in the investigation prior to the September 11 terrorist attack of Zacarias Moussaoui, the possible "20th hijacker" who did not make it onto an airplane because he was arrested before September 11, 2001, on immigration charges, the request by field agents to search his computer never made it past FBI attorneys, who found insufficient evidence to justify it.[149]

The Courts

Once surveillance technology is available that makes possible such actions as scanning e-mail or gaining the keys to decrypt messages, and once it is established in principle that the government will have access to such technology, the question for both sides becomes: under what conditions should the government be allowed to use it? Often, the contest on this second-level issue centers on the issuance of warrants and court orders.

Civil libertarians hold that court orders are issued too liberally, without due scrutiny. They argue that agents cannot be trusted to abide by minimization guidelines, so it is best not to grant them court orders in the first place. Jerry Berman stated that some 1,000 intercept orders a year are approved under FISA, suggesting that this is a very large number.[150] In fact, only around 10,000 intercept orders have been granted under FISA since its creation in 1979,[151] amounting to fewer than 1,000 a year.

Civil libertarians point to the fact that the FISC has only denied one request for surveillance in its entire history as evidence that the standards for receiving a FISA intercept order are lower than for receiving a Title III order.[152] Although applications for intercept orders are rarely turned down by the FISC, public safety advocates point out that it is embarrassing and damaging to one's record and career to be turned down by the FISC; and as a result, agents are reluctant to request warrants even when they seem justified.[153] Moreover, if the FISC finds that there is insufficient justification, it tends to return the request for further documentation rather than denying the request outright, which accounts for there being next to no outright refusals.[154] As mentioned, some requests never get past the Attorney General's Office. Also, FISA applications need to meet preset guidelines and must include a statement of the means by which the surveillance will be conducted, as well as a statement of proposed minimization procedures.[155]

Although civil libertarians typically are much more favorably disposed toward courts than toward the administrative parts of the government, they fear that judges might be unable or disinclined to curb law enforcement agents.[156] First, judges are either elected or politically appointed, making them subject to the influence of public opinion, especially since the September 11 terrorist attack. In addition, it has been suggested that judges are less accountable outside their home jurisdictions and might thus be less cautious in granting, and less diligent in enforcing proper implementation of, warrants and court orders that they issue that apply to other jurisdictions, as allowed by the USA PATRIOT Act. Judge Meskill, in his concurrence with the ruling in *United States v. Rodriguez*, warned that "judges may be more hesitant to authorize excessive interceptions within their territorial jurisdiction, in their own back yard so to speak, than in some distant, perhaps unfamiliar, part of the country. Congress determined that the best method of administering intercept authorizations included territorial limitation on the power of judges to make such authorizations."[157] If this is true, it would weaken the courts as an accountability mechanism for nationwide warrants.

In addition to the requirements that need to be met to get a warrant or court order in the first place, courts ensure that law enforcement agents act within the limits of the power granted to them by suppressing evidence that is collected illegally. The exclusionary rule—that evidence collected in violation of the Fourth Amendment must be excluded from a trial against the suspect—was not originally written into the Constitution but was established in the Supreme Court case *Boyd v. United States*[158] and later reaffirmed in *Weeks v. United States*.[159] It has since been diluted in more ways than one.[160] Still, evidence collected illegally will be suppressed. This serves not only to protect the suspect after a violation occurs but also to deter inappropriate searches because agents know that if they do not follow the correct procedures, the culprits might go free.

Congress

Under our system of checks and balances, Congress, of course, is supposed to oversee the work of the executive branch and its agencies. It has many instruments for doing so, including requiring heads of agencies and other high-ranking officials to respond to written questions, testify before congressional committees, and turn over documents; conducting hearings in which civil libertarians and others can make their case; ordering the General Accounting Office to conduct a study; and more.

A survey of the extent to which Congress provides another layer of accountability regarding issues such as those covered here, above and beyond what is provided by the agencies themselves and by the courts, is well beyond the scope of this chapter. It should be noted, however, that civil libertarians argue that many of the measures included in the

USA PATRIOT Act (including those explored here) were enacted in a great rush, without the usual hearings and deliberations.[161] Supporters of the public authorities point out that after the September 11 terrorist attack it was assumed that there were other "sleeper" terrorist agents in the United States and that other attacks were imminent, and they argue that therefore the rush was justified. Indeed, these supporters held that the government should have been granted expanded powers well before September 11, 2001.[162] Moreover, hearings and other reviews of the issues at hand, such as Carnivore, were conducted before September 11, 2001.[163] Thus, there were opportunities to explore the issues involved in such new security tools, and they were not simply rushed off the shelves into use after September 11, 2001.

The Public

The ultimate source of oversight is the citizenry, informed and alerted by a free press and civil liberties advocates and briefed by public authorities about their needs. To be fully effective in overseeing the issues at hand, civil libertarians argue that the public must be informed about the inner workings of the protective technologies, while public authorities claim that such disclosures would inform terrorists and other criminals about how to circumvent the technologies, thus rendering them useless. Specifically, since the existence of Carnivore was made public, numerous parties have demanded access to information about how it works. The ACLU filed a Freedom of Information Act (FOIA) request to get its source code, which reveals what a program is intended to do and how it operates.[164] The Electronic Privacy Information Center, a privacy advocacy group, filed an FOIA request to gain a copy of *all* documents relating to Carnivore.[165] In addition, numerous ISPs that might be asked to cooperate in installing Carnivore wanted guarantees that the program worked as claimed and that there would be sufficient controls to keep law enforcement agents from capturing more than what was covered in the court order.[166]

In the Scarfo case, the judge joined civil liberties groups in demanding that the FBI release information on how the KLS works, arguing that he could not rule on whether or not its use was legal without knowing how the technology worked. The judge said he would review the technology secretly.[167] This solution satisfied neither the civil libertarians nor the FBI. David Sobel of EPIC said that the matter raised "very basic questions of accountability. The suggestion that the use of high-tech law enforcement investigative techniques should result in a departure from our tradition of open judicial proceedings is very troubling."[168] Donald Kerr, assistant director of the FBI's laboratory division, stated that the disclosure of certain information about the KLS would "compromise the use of this technology . . . and jeopardize the safety of law enforcement personnel."[169]

Secrecy also remains one of the key objections to the use of roving intercepts under FISA. FISA was established in the mid-1970s, after the public was alarmed to learn of the activities of President Nixon and to discover that the NSA had been illegally intercepting telegraph and telephone calls.[170] A congressional committee was created to investigate, and found that nearly every president had authorized warrantless communications surveillance, often for political purposes.[171] Essentially, agencies such as the FBI, CIA, and NSA were able to conduct surveillance without going through normal criminal procedures. The Department of Justice launched its own in-house investigation, resulting in new guidelines for both domestic and foreign intelligence investigations. To prevent future abuses, Congress passed FISA in 1978 to spell out what the NSA (and other intelligence agencies) could and could not do.[172] The NSA had insisted that its activities—especially regarding its methods and technologies—would be severely compromised if discussed in open court. In response, FISA authorized the formation of a special federal court whose proceedings could be completely secret.[173]

In short, while the public cannot be informed about all the workings of all the protective technologies, such as Carnivore, because this would impair the usefulness of the technologies, the public can act as the ultimate enforcer of accountability.

Conclusion

To determine whether or not a specific public policy measure is legitimate entails more than establishing whether or not it significantly enhances public safety and is minimally intrusive, whether it further undermines already endangered civil rights, or makes it more difficult to deal with public needs. It entails rendering a judgment as to whether or not those who employ any new powers are sufficiently accountable to the various overseers—ultimately, the citizenry. Some powers are inappropriate no matter what oversight is provided. However, for those at issue here, the main question is whether there is sufficient accountability. *The remedy, if accountability is found deficient (or excessive), is to adjust accountability and not to deny the measure altogether.*

Whether the specific powers given to the government in regard to the matters at hand are sustaining or undermining the balance between rights and safety depends on how strong each layer of accountability is, whether higher layers enforce lower ones, and whether there are full complements of layers or not. It is true that there can be too much accountability, such that law enforcement agents would be reluctant to act due to fear that they would be penalized by superiors, by the courts, or by Congress, or be skewered by the press. However, there have been no signs of this since the September 11 terrorist attack.

Accountability is ultimately a matter of trust. Plato is said to have raised the issue in asking who will guard the guardians;[174] or, as it is put in Latin, *quis custodiet ipsos custodes?* Others attribute the question to the Roman satirist Juvenal, who wrote around 2000 years ago.[175] The issue, however, is still very much with us. If we do not trust the cops on the beat, we may ask their captains to keep them under closer supervision. If we do not trust the police, we may call on the civil authorities, such as mayors, to scrutinize the police. We may call on the other branches of government—the courts especially—to serve as checks and balances.

However, if we believe that the mayors are corrupt and the judges cannot be trusted either, then we have little to fall back on other than the fourth estate. Yet the media, too, is often distrusted.[176]

The question, then, is whom we should distrust and how much? If basically no authority or media figure is trustworthy and "The System" is corrupt, we face a much larger challenge than if, in a few instances, public authorities intercept more e-mail than they are supposed to, or tap some phones they ought not to. If someone believes this, she should either move to another country or fight for an entirely new political system.

In contrast, if only some cops, captains, mayors, and other public authorities are corrupt, we have good reason to watch out for such individuals, but not to doubt the political system. We ought, then, to work to improve the various layers of accountability, but also realize that the fact that critics can always come up with some horror stories does not necessarily mean that they are typical of the system.

Although I cannot justify it within the confines of this chapter, I hold the latter position. Hence, I suggest that one best ignores both claims by public authorities that no strengthening of accountability is needed and the shrillest civil libertarian outcries that sound as if no one is to be trusted. Instead, one is likely to favor reforms that will enhance accountability, rather than denying public authorities the tools they need to do their work (although not necessarily granting them all those they request) in a world in which new technologies have made their service more difficult and in which the threat to public safety has vastly increased.

4
Public Health and the Threat of Bioterrorism

Communitarian Bioethics

Before I proceed to explore the special implications of measures undertaken to enhance U.S. protection from bioterrorism, I need to revisit the communitarian position that was previously briefly introduced. It might be viewed as a synthesis that arises out of the contradictions of two previous systems of belief.

The "thesis" in this tri-legged dialectic evolution is the ultra social conservative position that the needs and values of the community or the society should trump individual considerations, and that the individual finds his or her purpose and meaning in serving the common good. Although there is room for individual choices, whenever these considerations of autonomy clash with the demands of the community, it is the community that ought to be privileged. This position is held by many East Asian leaders and intellectuals.[1] The notion that one can harvest organs without the consent of the person involved or their family is a bioethical derivative of this position.

The "antithesis," which historically arose in opposition to the ultra-social-conservative position, centers around the notion that individual rights should trump communal considerations. Autonomy (or liberty) is privileged. Although service to the common good has its place, it is best based on true and well-informed individual consent and choice, and on voluntary participation. Even persuasion and psychological pressure, not to mention economic inducement and coercion, are viewed as inappropriate under most circumstances.[2] Much of contemporary bioethics is, at least in part, based on this liberal political theory. Most obviously, the notion of informed consent is present not only in medical research (where the benefits accrue for the common good), but also in medical treatment (which is aimed at helping the individual).

Responsive (or new) communitarian thinking, from which my argument here will draw, is a synthesis of these two preceding approaches.[3] It takes as its starting point the concept that a good society is one in which there is a carefully crafted balance between autonomy and social order, between individual rights and social responsibilities. It does not privilege either individual or communal considerations, but views both as possessing valid moral claims.

Accordingly, communitarian thinking lays out the criteria from which one can formulate bioethical positions and public policies attentive to both the individual's claim to privacy and autonomy and the community's concern for public health and the trade offs involved. For instance, it rejects the position that each individual should decide on his or her own whether he or she wishes to be tested for HIV and disclose positive results to previous and prospective partners (the basic liberal position), as well as that people who are at high risk should be required to be tested and have the results disclosed (the ultra social conservative approach). The communitarian position can be articulated in terms of the following criteria, which can be applied to policy issues as a way to balance autonomy with social order. I developed this set of criteria based on my experience analyzing policy issues.[4] So far, they have been quite well received[5] and applied fairly extensively.[6] After introducing each criterion, I will provide a justification for its use in this chapter.

The first criterion suggests that one should not seek to modify existing ethical and legal standards unless there is a clear and present danger. The main reason is that such standards tend to unravel if they are wantonly or frequently recast, as they draw their legitimacy, in part, from their consistency over time. It is enough to imagine the Supreme Court overturning *Roe v. Wade* or any other matter of importance to see how damaging such frequent changes can be. The same holds for a religious authority such as the Pope or a chief rabbi who changes his or her ruling often. That which constitutes a clear and present danger may include anything that threatens a large number of people, let alone a whole society, race, or other grouping. For instance, genocide would qualify. HIV meets this criterion as hundreds of thousands of people die each year from the disease; Ebola, currently, does not, as few, if any, people contract the disease and die from it.

The second criterion is whether or not the challenge at hand can be treated effectively by voluntary means. Voluntary means are to be preferred for two reasons. First because, by definition, they do not entail changing the constitution and basic laws, which, to reiterate, benefits the country. Also, the best way to reduce the tension between autonomy and the common good is to convince people to take needed health measures on their own. The reason, spelled out elsewhere, is that all coercive measures—even if undertaken for a worthy purpose, even solely for the individual's benefit—leave a share of resentment and alienation.[7] In contrast, acts that individuals are truly persuaded to undertake on their own, even if they only serve the common good, become their preferences and do not leave resentment or alienation in their wake. For instance, people who do not smoke in public because they truly are convinced that such behavior is inappropriate are typically not troubled by bans on such smoking. This is also true for HIV testing and disclosure; for example, once select gay leaders championed it and, to the extent that it became a norm in several gay communities, it became successful.

(In contrast, given no such community, leadership, and norms, persuasion has had very limited effects on intravenous drug users who exchange needles.)

The third criterion follows logically from the first two, but it only comes into play when there is a clear and present danger and voluntary means do not suffice. It entails using minimally coercive means because they serve the common good, while violating as little autonomy as possible. For instance, imposing penalties on those persons who knew that their HIV status was positive and did not warn their partners or had unprotected sex is justified not only for the sake of the individual who might be infected with an always fatal disease, but also for the common good that will be damaged if the spread of the disease is not curbed.

The fourth criterion is not based on any high principles, communitarian or otherwise, but rather on sociological findings: no matter how carefully we plan ahead and proceed, our policies will tend to have unintended side effects. We need to be aware of them and be ready to deal with them. Thus for instance, if changes in the law lead more people to be tested for HIV, those involved ought to take special pains to ensure that test results remain confidential.

Before these criteria are applied to bioterrorism, it should be noted that there is a tendency to confuse new communitarianism with authoritarian communitarianism and suspect that it privileges communities over individual rights. It should hence be noted that the four criteria just outlined can be and have been used to point to situations in which liberty needs to be strengthened rather than made to service the common good. This was effectively demonstrated in a study of medical privacy conducted by applying the four said criteria. It led to the conclusion that, in the 1990s, medical privacy was violated by private parties without any clear and present danger, and without benefit for the common good. Furthermore, whatever public service these private actors claimed to have provided (especially for medical research and public safety) could have been achieved by means that did not violate privacy (or autonomy). This communitarian study, published in 1999, outlined a list of measures to be undertaken to correct the existing imbalance between privacy and the social order—by moving toward privacy.[8] Many of the long list of regulations to protect medical privacy that were promulgated by the federal government in 2000/2001 and took effect in 2002, follow similar guidelines.[9]

Criteria for Judging Responses to Bioterrorism

Clear and Present Danger

As often is the case with new threats, the scope of the dangers posed by terrorism is very difficult to assess. Although one can assign various probabilities to the possibility that the nation will be subject to a major act of biological terrorism, these probabilities are based largely on speculation. Moreover, the scope of the threat varies immensely according to which agents are expected to be used (e.g., how infectious they are), how proficiently they are produced (e.g., if they have been modified to resist treatment, are two or more agents combined, or are they newly designed "super bugs") how easy they are to deliver and spread, how difficult they are to detect, and so on.[10] In proceeding, it is crucial to realize that both the probability of an attack and the magnitude of its potential severity must be considered. Even if it were somehow reliably known that the probability of a bioterrorist attack was very low, the negative outcome of such an attack could be very great: attackers could use agents that are very infectious, easy to spread, difficult to detect, modified to prevent treatment, and might result in high fatality rates.[11] Because of this potentially disastrous consequence, one must conclude that we face a clear and present danger.

Voluntary, Educational Means

The preferred voluntary means for responding to the threat of a bioterrorist attack can inform several policies. One concerns the introduction of preventive vaccines. Some favor vaccinating Americans against smallpox to protect them from an agent that is highly contagious and has a very high fatality rate. Beyond that, the former executive director of the American Public Health Association, Dr. Mohammad Akhter, has suggested that consideration should be given to vaccinate Americans against several other potential agents.[12]

Preventive vaccinations raise several ethical and policy issues. First, all vaccinations pose a risk. For smallpox, Tara O'Toole of the Center for Biosecurity at the University Pittsburgh Medical Center estimated that one in 300,000 persons would die from the vaccine or suffer irreversible brain damage as a result of it. Thus, if all Americans were vaccinated, approximately 1,000 persons would die or suffer the said adverse side-effects.[13] The information about side effects of the vaccination against anthrax is less clear. The Centers for Disease Control's National Immunization Program estimates that serious allergic reactions to the anthrax vaccine are less than one in 100,000 cases and the risk of causing serious harm or death is "extremely small."[14] The Department of Defense reports that about one in 200,000 persons have adverse reactions to the vaccine that require hospitalization.[15]

Vaccines also vary in their effectiveness. In the case of smallpox, a single dose of the vaccine is generally thought to be highly effective for 10 years, although some studies claim the vaccine is effective for a longer period of time.[16] In a study the World Health Organization cites of smallpox cases in Europe and Canada between 1951 and 1970, mortality was 52 percent for unvaccinated persons, while it was 1.4 percent for persons vaccinated within the past 10 years.[17] The vaccine helped health professionals eradicate the disease in the late 1970s. In contrast, the basic anthrax vaccine, as given by the Department of Defense to military personnel, consists of a series of six doses—spread over some 18 months—and annual booster shots thereafter.[18] Furthermore, the efficacy of the vaccine against anthrax in general, and against inhaled anthrax in particular, is questionable.[19]

Is urging people to be voluntarily vaccinated a justifiable measure, given the risks to which individuals will be exposed, compared with the public's gain? Neither mathematical formulas nor highly specific ethical principles apply. However, from a communitarian perspective, *both* the size of the risks to the person and the size of the contribution to the community must be taken into account. Beyond that, a principle often used in law applies: what would the reasonable person do? Given that the smallpox vaccination's risks are very small and the potential public gain is enormous, this vaccination is justified. In contrast, given that anthrax is not contagious (and hence vaccination against it has little communal value, other than the protection of those directly involved) and its efficacy is dubious, it seems that urging this vaccination on people is not justified at this stage.

It should be noted in passing that it may seem at first that given the fact that vaccines protect the individual at hand, calling for them (if the risks are low) could be justified strictly on individualistic grounds. This might be the case for a traveler who is setting out to visit a country in which a given infection is rampant. However, when an entire population is vaccinated, the standard free rider rationale applies. It would serve each individual well if all other people were to be vaccinated. This way, an individual could avoid the vaccine and any danger it may pose and still be protected. (Indeed, under the circumstances, it would make little sense for a terrorist to attack a population with the same agent from which much of the public is protected, making the choice of avoiding the vaccinations even more "rational" for the individual involved.) Therefore, choosing to be vaccinated entails a considerable commitment to the common good. Hence, when encouraging people to be vaccinated against whatever agents one concludes are dangerous, it is best to take into account that one must appeal to people's civic duty, and not merely to their own interests, lest they point out that if they were guided by only self-centered considerations, they would likely not come forward.

Vaccinations should be preceded by massive public health education campaigns to maximize voluntary acceptance. However, one must expect that a fair number of individuals will not voluntarily come forward. Compliance research shows that numerous individuals are disinclined to ever attend to matters that directly benefit their own health, even if no significant risks, costs, or efforts are involved—for instance, taking their medication regularly. In addition, there are ideological objections from libertarians and civil libertarians to the paternalism involved, while others are driven by paranoid theories about the government's intentions,[20] and still others—as we know from experience with childhood vaccinations against measles—are motivated by free rider considerations.[21]

Public education campaigns hence must often be backed up by other measures. Communitarian analysis suggests that given the small "costs" to the individual and the high public gain, the application of social pressure is justified and works best to the extent that people are members of communities (are "embedded")[22] and their leaders— of churches, for example—can be mobilized to support the endeavor. (This contrasts with campaigns that focus on trying directly to reach each individual.)

Few object to positive social pressure (encouraging people to comply); however, as a rule, this does not suffice. Hence, negative social pressures must also be considered if a sufficiently high level of vaccination is to be achieved. Shaming is most effective. For instance, listing on communal bulletin boards or web pages those who fail to pay child support or taxes will increase the compliance rate.

Shaming (and other forms of negative social pressures, from giving students failing grades to sports that "bench" players who are less prepared) evokes considerable objections from those who fear that it will damage people's self-esteem or be otherwise abusive. However, shaming is not coercive, both in the sense that no physical force is applied and that the ultimate decision is left in the hands of the actor. Above all, it compares favorably to other measures that might have to be used, especially if without it an insufficient level of compliance will be attained.[23]

Economic pressures are much more difficult to entertain because they place a higher burden on the less endowed than on those who are affluent—for instance, requiring workers to show up with vaccination certificates or be denied that day's pay. These are still preferable to actual coercive measures, such as stopping people on streets and vaccinating them on the spot if they have no documentation.

Coercive Measures

When are massive coercive measures justified? Whether it is justified for a population to be subject to fully mandatory vaccination and coercive steps to (even following a bioterrorist attack) depends a great deal on the nature of the agent and scope of the attack. For instance, the 2001 anthrax attack in the United States and a bioterror act before it in Oregon (in which a cult contaminated salad bars with salmonella)[24] were small in scale, were not contagious, had low fatality rates, involved diseases that could be readily treated if detected early, and were relatively easy to detect. Indeed, the anthrax attack caused more alarm than actual harm to the public. In retrospect, it might be seen as a helpful wake-up call to a nation unprepared to deal with bioterrorism.

When considering a more severe bioterrorist attack, much of the respective responses that can be justified depends on highly specific details. For instance, it makes a world of difference whether or not the agent has been "weaponized," whether or not there is a period in which symptoms are visible before those infected become contagious, and so on. In the following analysis, the discussion follows a scenario often used before, that of a smallpox attack.[25] It cannot be sufficiently reiterated that, although the criteria of analysis will not change, the conclusions could be different if the specific nature of the attack varied from the one assumed in this scenario. For the sake of this analysis, it is assumed that the attack has occurred in numerous places simultaneously, that symptoms are detected a few days before the person becomes contagious, that most of the population has not been vaccinated, and that the expected fatality rate is as high as 30 percent.

Following such an attack, fully mandatory vaccination of the uninfected population (at least in the areas surrounding the populations that have been infected) seems justified given the low risk to the persons involved and the high gains to the public. (This presumes that sufficient vaccine is available and viable[26] and that the evidence continues to show that even if those who are vaccinated become infected, their illness will be less severe.)[27]

Additional coercive measures are called for if preventive vaccinations have not been undertaken, given that post-hoc vaccination is, at best, not fully effective. The most important action to take is isolation of those infected.[28] Such a separation amounts to a quarantine of one form or another. From a communitarian viewpoint, quarantining is fully justified on the grounds that many millions of Americans (and millions of others) will otherwise die following a debilitating illness, while the intrusion on the autonomy of those segregated could be made quite small. In the case of smallpox, a quarantine can be limited to roughly 17 days, after which time those involved cease to be contagious.[29]

Quarantining has historically been used often, most recently in Yugoslavia in 1972 when a pilgrim returning from Iraq contracted smallpox. In response, neighboring countries closed their borders to Yugoslavia, in effect quarantining the country.[30] The country also had to deal with numerous people who were in contact with others who had contracted smallpox. Persons were quarantined for a period of two weeks in hotels, cordoned off by fences and police. In the meantime, the country vaccinated its entire population of 19 million persons. Eight weeks after the first case of smallpox, the outbreak ended with 175 smallpox cases and 35 deaths.[31] It is widely considered an outbreak that the nations involved handled effectively.

In the United States, quarantining seems to bring to many minds the image of dirty barracks in some desolate place, or the indignities of Ellis Island, or worse yet, the dust ridden places Japanese Americans were detained during World War II. For some others, it even evokes the image of leper colonies. However, there is no reason why a quarantine should be in such locations. First of all, it would need to be centered around medical facilities. Second, it would need to include a whole row of hotels to accommodate the many thousands of people who will need to be housed and treated, as most are going to be quite ill. Indeed, there is no reason why a quarantine could not be placed, say, at beach resorts or vacation islands. In fact, given how intrusive and traumatic a quarantine would be, I would argue that the government should make conditions as hospitable as possible under the circumstances.

Quarantining: A Liberal Tilt and a Communitarian Correction

Before, and occasionally after, the September 11 terrorist attack, quarantining was stigmatized, which was reflected in the ways it was treated in relevant discussions of bioethics, public health policies, and measures to cope with bioterrorism. Jessica Stern, who teaches public policy at Harvard's Kennedy School of Government, discusses in her 1999 book, *The Ultimate Terrorists*,[32] numerous measures that should be taken in preparation for terrorist attacks. Preparing the legal grounds under which quarantining might be undertaken and sorting out the issues involved is not so much as mentioned.

Donald Henderson, a leading authority on bioterrorism, who was the director of the Health and Human Services Department's Office of Public Health Preparedness, testified before Congress (September 5, 2001) on preventing the use of biological weapons and on improving a response to them if used.[33] Quarantining was not mentioned.

A leading legal scholar, Larry Gostin, has worked extensively on these issues, and in a book published prior to September 11, 2001, he dedicates a chapter to "Restrictions of the Person" and frames the issue in the typical liberal way (rather than calling the chapter, say, "How to Save Millions of Lives with Minimal Intrusion").[34] He provides a brief history of quarantines and similar measures. He points out that three criteria were used to establish the legality of quarantines: the disease must actually be infectious; there must be a safe and healthy environment in which the confinement may take place; and it may not be exercised on racial or other discriminatory grounds.[35] By these criteria, smallpox confinement could be readily justified. But Gostin goes on to report that constitutional doctrine has changed so drastically since the 1960s that he greatly doubts that earlier justifications of quarantining would hold today and that now rights to travel would be given much greater weight than in the past; quarantining would be considered a "massive curtailment of liberty."[36] Gostin has been working on a model law that states should adopt in order to implement quarantining if there were "compelling public interest."

The reasons quarantining has either not been considered or mentioned only with considerable hesitancy are numerous. In part, the leading figures in contemporary political theory, social philosophy, ethics, and bioethics in the United States tend to be on the liberal side. John Rawls, for instance, is often cited as the most influential philosopher of the day. As mentioned in the introduction to this volume, even conservatives such as Congressmen Bob Barr and Dick Armey and organizations such as Phyllis Schlafly's Eagle Forum have expressed concerns similar to those expressed by the American Civil Liberties Union and Common Cause. Both liberal and conservative groups have joined in a coalition of more than 150 organizations to protect individual rights after the September 11 terrorist attack.[37] Major newspapers, National Public Radio, and public television tend to take the position that the onus for any deferment or recalibration of rights is on the advocates of public safety. Measures are subjected to strict scrutiny and are often deemed overly broad.

But this was not always the case. During the first 190 years of the republic, public policies reflected a predominant concern for social order. During this time, the government often neglected rights (and readily employed quarantining).[38] However, many of the core values and institutions that undergirded the old social order were undermined in the 1960s by various liberation movements (e.g., civil rights, women, youth, sexual, and counterculture). Given that the old regime was discriminatory against minorities and women, as well as somewhat authoritarian, there is good reason to celebrate its demise. As mentioned previously in regard to the FBI and the Church Commission, in effect, the 1960s might well be viewed as a major communitarian correction— moving in the liberal direction, away from excessive and oppressive social order toward a better balance.

During the following years, American society over-corrected, crossing the line from shored up liberties to a moral anomie. As few new shared values and institutions have arisen to fill the vacuum generated by the undercutting of the old ones, the society has moved toward what Alan Wolfe called "moral freedom"[39] and others might consider a moral free-for-all. Robert Bellah and his associates showed that the period of excessive individualism (led by the counterculture) was followed by a period of instrumental individualism (the rise of neoconservatism, libertarianism, and the Reagan years of watching out for Numero Uno).[40]

Finally, and most relevant for the context in which early 21st century biodefense measures are being considered, Ronald Bayer has shown in his masterful book, *Private Acts, Social Consequences*,[41] that social restrictions intended to promote public health (a common good par excellence), and quarantining in particular, became much less acceptable following the increase in HIV infection and the concurrent rise in political awareness and activity of gay groups. Thus, the quarantine of people with HIV, which was routine in Cuba, was not even discussable in the United States. (I am not suggesting that it was called for, but merely reporting that it has been shown that before the rise in HIV, quarantining in the United States was quite acceptable, and even today is used for people who have active tuberculosis; but that since the outbreak of AIDS, it has been stigmatized.[42]) Reinforcing each other, all these normative, cultural, social, and political changes led to a sense that massive coercion, entailed in mass quarantine, was beyond the pale.

The preceding communitarian analysis suggests that a correction favoring the common good to the previous liberal tilt is needed, given the recent increased levels of threats to the public's health. Already there is hope that the U.S. government will again consider the use of quarantine as an effective treatment option. During the 2003 SARS outbreak, the Centers for Disease Control recommended, but did not require, the quarantine of those who fell ill with the highly contagious respiratory disease.[43] SARS prompted other places such as Buffalo, New York and Minnesota to develop strategic plans to quarantine victims of an outbreak or bioterror attack, including the establishment of a legal appeals process for individuals who did not want to be quarantined.[44] As of November 2001, such a correction has been setting in. Cities and states rushed to introduce legislation that would authorize banning public events, commandeering hotels, and quarantining millions of people. Such moves are best accompanied by public education to justify them. Donald Henderson called for educating people about the nature and symptoms of a disease so that they can recognize it should they become infected. Depending on the agent, they should seek treatment and/or voluntarily remove themselves from the population-at-large.[45] Similarly, officials in the Washington, D.C. area are creating a self-triage website, which includes a series of questions followed by recommendations to either "stay home in voluntary quarantine, go to a designated site for follow-up care, move to an isolation facility, or just relax."[46]

Also called for is a reexamination of the prevailing conceptual and ethical frameworks provided by public intellectuals and academics, especially by bioethicists and social philosophers. There is a danger that without such public persuasion and a reframing of the debate—if the adjustment of law and policy will continue to take place under panic, especially following a major attack—public authorities will overcorrect, as we have seen in other areas (e.g., the way military tribunals have been initially introduced and structured). In the current climate, in which two-thirds of the public supports waiving many rights,[47] we may end up forcing unjustified vaccinations against numerous agents (as already has been indirectly called for by the American Public Health Association)[48] and isolating, without rhyme or reason, travelers from countries that we suspect have been exposed to biological agents. Communitarian thinking might help call attention to our tendency to oversteer and the need to keep a carefully crafted balance between autonomy and the common good.

In short, communitarianism does not rule out the use of coercion (as most laws entail), but treats it as a last resort. It finds a place only when persuasion and economic incentives turn out to be insufficient. When coercion is applied, it must be minimally intrusive. Above all, rather than one-sided advocacy of autonomy and rights clashing with one-sided advocacy of public order, communitarian analysis privileges neither side and is forever leery of over-corrections.

Agency: The Role of Public Health Authorities

Assuming one grants that the threat of bioterrorism justifies some measures of favoring public health over unfettered attention to individual rights, for instance in preparing the legal ground for massive quarantining, the question arises as to which agency is best suited to implement the new measures.

Laurie Garrett, a Pulitzer Prize winning author whose volumes on this subject are often cited, is deeply concerned that the agencies involved would include the Federal Bureau of Investigation (FBI) or the military, rather than public health authorities.[49] She fears that the FBI will focus on determining who the culprit is rather than on preventing the spread of the disease. Indeed, there is some reason for such concern. In 1997 the office of B'nai B'rith in Washington, D.C., received an envelope that contained suspicious materials. The emergency medical team treated the building as a hot zone. They subjected all occupants to showers on the street to ensure that they would not carry infectious agents out of the perimeter of the hot zone. However, when the police arrived on the scene, they treated it as a crime scene and marched in and out of the hot zone, refusing to shower.[50] There is little reason to doubt that each agency has a distinct culture and structure, divergent habits and missions, and is governed by distinct regulations. Hence, the question of which agency, or what combination of agencies, should lead when dealing with bioterrorism deserves attention.

Garrett argues for the maintenance of a social contract, one in which individuals disclose information for the sake of the community's health, and public health authorities protect the privacy of patients.[51] Hence, she strongly favors giving public health authorities a dominant role in dealing with the after-effects of an attack rather than having the police, National Guard, or the military singlehandedly dictate the course of action.[52]

Garrett's books and articles were published before September 11, 2001. Since then we have learned that the FBI, whose task it is to determine who the culprits are, was able to restrain itself and allow priority to be given to saving lives in rescue operations at the Pentagon and World Trade Center, rather than controlling those sites as crime scenes, even well after the probability of saving lives became very low. The National Guard, involved in protecting airports, has not been observed to have acted with undue disrespect for individual rights. One may also wonder whether the relatively liberal culture of the Centers for Disease Control will make it too reluctant to call for the coercive measures that might be needed.

Much of the work that does not involve coercion would seem to fit well with the missions of public health authorities. The work that involves coercion could be overseen and guided by public health authorities, although they may have to be backed up by local police forces, and quite likely the National Guard and possibly the military. This means that the time has come to increase greatly the resources and authority of the public health service.

In either case, whether the public health service is in charge or merely a major partner in dealing with the preparations and responses to a massive bioterrorist attack, one must deal with the effects of decades of downgrading the public health service. Once it was considered the leading agency in improving people's health by overcoming infectious diseases and improving the hygiene of food and water and beaches. Indeed, it was credited with having significantly more achievements in improving people's health than private medical care.[53] However, following the spread of antibiotics, administered largely by private physicians and hospitals, the rise of fee-for-service medical care, and the conservative ideology that favors minimizing the government (including health services) and budgets (which, for public health, was cut some 25 percent between 1981 and 1993),[54] the prestige of working for public health has declined.[55] As a result, its employees are often not the most highly regarded or the best qualified, to put it mildly.

Within the realm of public health, both the budget and prestige have been concentrated on the National Institutes of Health, where research is conducted, and on the Centers for Disease Control, in which research and surveillance is carried out, but not on state and local health departments and authorities. Moreover, public health services are highly divided among thousands of jurisdictions and entities with inconsistent regulations and powers, thus making concerted efforts almost impossible.[56]

It is now clear that preparing for bioterrorist attacks cannot adequately be carried out by private health agents (e.g., by merely relying on teaching doctors and hospitals to recognize the symptoms and allowing them to treat the patients), assuming that there may well be a massive attack with infectious agents. Indeed, the very fact that an attack is brewing requires the collection of information (e.g., say a sudden increase in flu-like symptoms or pet deaths) and monitoring of that information, which only public health agencies have the authority to enforce.

One may argue that many of these missions could be delegated to profit-making firms, although they would need massive public funds. (e.g., to carry out public education), and physicians and hospitals would be required to collaborate with such firms (e.g., to collect and disclose information). In July, 2004, Congress was close to passing legislation that would provide the pharmaceutical industry with ". . . the financial guarantees it says it needs to research and produce vaccines and antidotes for bioterror agents that otherwise would have little marketable value." Jim Abrams, "Congress Nears OK of Weapons Ban," *Associated Press*, 14 July 2004. There is no need to rehash the arguments about the relative merit of public service via the private versus the public sector—the sort that have recently taken place regarding airport security. For the sake of the issue at hand, it should be noted that in either case a very substantial increase in public funding, staff, and enforcement powers is called for. Also, the experience with for-profit prisons, mental hospitals, and nursing homes (all areas of human services) is not particularly reassuring. It is difficult to imagine a private health-providing firm coordinating the activities of the FBI, police, National Guard, and military following an attack.

Building up public health involves changes in all areas in which deficits have occurred: budget, quality of staff, regulatory authority, coordination, and the balance between research and service components. Such changes amount to a major correction in favor of the common good—those directly dedicated to the well-being of the community. They are not centered around improving the prospects of this or that individual, as the fee for service system is, but on improving the general conditions from which the public draws. For example, it protects resources (e.g., water reservoirs) that are not the property of any one individual or even an aggregate of individuals, but of the community, including children not yet born and future generations. For more, see Amitai Etzioni, *The Common Good* (Cambridge, U.K.: Polity Press, 2004).

For those who subscribe to the communitarian analysis that holds that by the end of the 20th century American society was neglecting the common good, shoring up public health is a reaction to terrorism that differs from most others that we have seen to date. Most other preparations—from cement barriers to air marshals, from new machines that inspect the mail to curtailments of our legal rights—are not merely a heavy cost to bear, but are wasted if no future attack occurs. In contrast, strengthening public health would be in the community's interest even if no further acts of terrorism were to occur.

5

A Case for National ID Cards?

Reliable Identification Is Essential for Homeland Protection

The prevalence of means of identification that are easily falsified or are obtained in a fraudulent manner is a particularly vulnerable element of the homeland security of the United States. Unless these means of identification are substantially improved, many new systems such as the U.S. visitor and immigrant status indication technology program (U.S. VISIT), which has replaced the suspended national security entry exit registration system (NSEERS) and encompasses the foreign student tracking system (SEVIS), the airline passenger screening system (CAPPS II), as well as current watch lists maintained by the FBI, the CIA, and the U.S. Citizenship and Immigration Services (USCIS), and many other programs that help protect the public will continue to be severely hampered.

Press reports suggest that the reluctance of the White House and Congress to deal with the means by which people are identified stems from concerns that an action taken in this area would entail the introduction of a national ID card,[1] which faces strong opposition from the left and right and from many in the public.[2]

The opposition to national ID cards reflects four general concerns. First, there is the concern of those who oppose national ID cards because of their historical association with totalitarian governments. Robert Ellis Smith, publisher of *Privacy Journal*, has warned that issuing national ID cards would be comparable to "the Nazi experience in Europe,"[3] and the American Civil Liberties Union (ACLU) has called them "a primary tool of totalitarian governments to restrict the freedoms of their citizens."[4] Another concern that others express is that national ID cards are an assault on personal privacy. This view is championed by a wide coalition of the left and the right, including groups ranging from the ACLU to Phyllis Schlafly's pro-family Eagle Forum. These groups are most concerned with the access to personal information that national ID cards grant to the government. Schlafly, one of the more outspoken opponents of national ID cards, has argued that "[p]utting all that information on a government database means the end of privacy as we know it. Daily actions we all take for granted will henceforth be recorded, monitored, tracked, and contingent on showing The Card."[5]

A third concern is that the cards are a potential "slippery slope." Groups such as the Cato Institute argue that even if national ID cards are not immediate precursors to a totalitarian state, they open the door for future governments to ease the safeguards associated with the ID cards and expand their scope, which could eventually usher in a more intrusive government.[6] These groups often cite the fact that Social Security cards were originally conceived to serve a specific purpose, but have since become far more prevalent as a means of identification.

Finally, there is the concern that such forms of identification will make it easier for employers and government officials to discriminate against minorities. For instance, some have cautioned that officials might insist on seeing the ID cards of "foreign-looking" citizens based on unfounded suspicions.[7]

I do not recommend such a course of action. My concern here is with what I call *purposive* means of identification; that is, means issued by governments and by private industry for specific purposes. People are not required to carry these means of identification with them at all times or to show them upon demand, as is the case with national ID cards used in other countries, such as Belgium and Spain. Many different types of purposive means of identification (not necessarily cards) are used by people when they seek to *access controlled areas*, such as airplanes, secure facilities, most public buildings, and numerous private ones. For the 40 million foreigners who travel to the United States each year for vacation, to attend school, or to conduct business,[8] the United States itself is a controlled area. To enter it, people are required to identify themselves. Therefore, the United States should not rely on any one means of identification, but rather it should utilize multiple means of identification, depending upon the purposes at hand and the desired level of security (compare, for instance, someone obtaining a library card at a local public library with someone obtaining a credential that allows him or her to transport hazardous materials across the country).

Means of identification developed for one purpose are sometimes widely used for others, which generates both some difficulties and considerable benefits. This is most prominently the case for driver's licenses, which were originally issued for traffic safety, but often have been used for identifying people who seek to cash checks and, prominently in the last years, for homeland security purposes. These different usages require different levels of reliability; however, driver's licenses have not been adapted to meet the higher level of security needed for the war against terrorism. The same holds true for any other means of identification created for one purpose and used for others. The subtext of much of what follows is how to deal with the issues that arise from such mission creep.

Next, I show in some detail that many of the means of identification routinely used in the United States are still highly unreliable. All three elements of how individuals are identified—the processes, personnel, and technologies involved—need to be improved to make means of identification more reliable.

Means of identification cannot be made foolproof, but very substantial improvements can be made that will greatly enhance our security and will have what I call collateral gains; that is, they will introduce ways to help treat other serious national problems.

The format of this chapter differs from previous ones. Here I first discuss how it would help national security to make means of identification more reliable for those who wish out of their own free will to enter controlled areas. These means of identification differ from national ID cards (which one must by law have on one's person at all times and present on demand even without any special reason to be identified). They hence raise relatively few rights issues. Toward the end of the chapter I point out that more reliable identification *helps* conserve privacy, because authorities will need less information about a person to determine his or her identity. And I discuss the development of various accountability and oversight measures to ensure that more reliable forms of identification will not be abused.

Unreliable Means of Identification Severely Hamper Homeland Security

This section presents evidence in support of the observation that despite some recent improvements, the prevailing means of identification, which are commonly relied upon in the United States, are woefully inadequate.

Border Security: One Hundred Percent Failure Rate

Mr. Robert J. Cramer, managing director at the General Accounting Office's (GAO) Office of Special Investigations (OSI), testified before the House of Rereratatives that an investigation of the GAO conducted between September 2002 and May 2003 found that in every instance— without a single exception—when agents attempted to enter the United States from Western Hemisphere countries using counterfeit driver's licenses and birth certificates with fake identities, they were successful.

The border patrol agents failed to realize that the documents were not authentic. For the security tests, OSI agents used widely available computer graphics software to create counterfeit documents; in other words, they used material that could be found in an average home. In the course of this investigation, OSI agents used counterfeit documents and false identities to enter the United States from four countries. It is important to keep in mind that U.S. citizens—or people claiming to be U.S. citizens—seeking to enter the United States from Western Hemisphere countries are not required to show a passport to enter the United States; instead, they are required to prove American citizenship. This may be done through a state-issued birth certificate or a baptismal record, and photo identification, for instance a driver's license, or, as the GAO notes, "since the law does not require that U.S. citizens who enter the United States from Western Hemisphere countries present documents to prove citizenship they are permitted to establish U.S. citizenship by oral statements alone."[9] Teams of two OSI agents tried to enter the United States from Canada three times, from Mexico two times, from Jamaica one time, and from Barbados one time; and each time agents were able to cross the border—whether at an airport, a land border crossing, or a sea port of entry—and border patrol agents failed to recognize that the documents that the undercover agents were using were counterfeit.[10]

Federal Buildings and Airports: Highly Porous

In April and May 2000, the GAO's OSI agents tried to gain access to nineteen federal buildings and two airports using counterfeit law enforcement credentials (that were either acquired from public sources or were created using commercial software packages, information from the Internet, and an ink-jet color printer). Agents gained entry into eighteen of the twenty-one sites on their first attempt; they entered the other three sites on their second attempt. Thus, at all sites the agents were successful and the counterfeit documents were not detected. The facilities in which the agents gained entry were not minor ones, but rather included some of the most sensitive and, presumably, most secure facilities, such as the CIA, the Pentagon, the FBI, the Department of State, the Department of Justice, and others.[11]

Upon entering the "secure" buildings or the airport terminals, the undercover agents, carrying counterfeit credentials, declared that they were armed law enforcement officials and were able to pass through security without being screened. Robert H. Hast, assistant comptroller general for investigations with the OSI, reported to the House of Representatives that "at the 21 sites that our undercover agents successfully penetrated, they could have carried in weapons, listening devices, explosives, chemical/biological agents, devices, and/or other such items/ materials," since one agent always carried a valise.[12]

Another troubling finding was that at fifteen of the sixteen facilities where agency heads or cabinet secretaries worked, agents were able to stand directly outside their suites. The five times agents attempted to enter the suites, they were able to do so successfully. Undercover agents also were able to enter restrooms near the agency head's or cabinet secretary's suite and could have left dangerous materials there without being detected.[13]

Airport officials did not detect the counterfeit documents either. Airline ticket agents readily gave the undercover OSI agents "law enforcement" boarding passes. Although the procedures for getting through security varied at the two airports, none of the agents nor their valises were screened by security personnel.[14]

In response to these findings, nineteen of the twenty-one agencies and airports that were part of the original GAO study responded that they had taken specific actions to enhance their security in the wake of the findings.[15] However, since then, a task force investigation into Washington, D.C. area airports immediately following September 11, 2001, revealed that those airports' general security systems remain lax. The task force, formed by U.S. Attorney Paul McNulty of the Eastern District of Virginia, examined the records of airport employees who held Security Identification Display Area badges, which allow access to secured areas of Dulles International and Reagan National Airports.[16]

McNulty reported to the House of Representatives that the investigation found that "75 airport workers used false or fictitious social security account numbers to obtain security badges and that afforded them unescorted access into the most sensitive areas of our airports."[17] He went on to say that "Many of these airport workers also used the same false or fictitious social security number to obtain Virginia driver's licenses, fill out immigration forms, or apply for credit cards."[18]

The Washington area airports were not alone in having individuals use fraudulent identifiers to obtain security passes. After the September 11 terrorist attacks, a Department of Justice investigation into employees at the Salt Lake City International Airport found that "61 individuals with the highest-level security badges and 125 with lower level badges . . . misused SSN's" to obtain security badges or fill out employment eligibility forms.[19]

Military Facilities: Like an Open Book

When the GAO's OSI agents used false means of identification (a fake ID card from a fictitious agency within the Department of Defense), they even were able to enter areas controlled by the military, areas in which weapons are stored as they are shipped across the country. Moreover, the undercover agents were allowed unhampered access to the weapons themselves. The GAO report on this matter has apparently proven either so damaging to national security or so embarrassing to the government, or both, that it has been withdrawn from circulation.[20]

Entering the United States

Immigration and Naturalization Service (INS) officials intercepted more than one hundred thousand fraudulent documents annually between fiscal years 1999 and 2001. These documents included border crossing cards, nonimmigrant visas, alien registration cards, U.S. and foreign passports and citizen documents, as well as other documents.[21] While every intercept of a fraudulent document is a success, many are not detected. This is evidenced by the fact that in a twenty-month period between October 1996 and May 1998, the INS reported that "about 50,000 unauthorized aliens were found to have used 78,000 fraudulent documents to obtain employment."[22]

It is impossible to assess to what extent this problem has been alleviated since September 11, but the following reports suggest that it is far from resolved. Raids in the Seattle area in September 2002 netted enough computer equipment and specialty paper to print more than eight hundred fraudulent documents, including driver's licenses, Social Security cards, green cards, and Mexican driver's licenses.[23] In Washington, D.C., raids resulting from an ongoing investigation that began in April 2002 have netted more than one thousand fraudulent documents and nearly fifty arrests.[24] In one bust during this ongoing investigation, authorities confiscated more than five hundred fake residency cards, Social Security cards, driver's licenses, and other IDs at a single residence. Cynthia O'Connell, Acting Director of the Identity Fraud Unit of the Bureau of Immigration and Customs Enforcement, reported in August 2003 that "there are not enough agents to do it all, especially after 9/11."[25]

Terrorists Too

Many of the September 11 hijackers and their associates have been found to have used counterfeit Social Security numbers (ones that were never issued by the Social Security Administration [SSA]). Meanwhile, one of the hijackers used the Social Security number of a child, and other hijackers used numbers that had been associated with multiple names.[26] This fake or counterfeit information seems to have been used by the hijackers to obtain driver's licenses. Some of the hijackers held multiple licenses from states including Virginia, Florida, California, Arizona, and Maryland. Only one of the hijackers appeared not to possess a state-issued form of ID, according to Senator Richard Durbin at his hearing on driver's licenses in April 2002.[27] Additionally, Timothy McVeigh used a fake ID to rent the Ryder van that exploded in front of the Murrah Federal Building in Oklahoma City in April 1995.[28]

In short, the urgent need for more reliable means of identification for homeland security is evident. New systems such as U.S. VISIT and older systems such as watch lists are not useless; however, these systems would become much more effective if the processes of issuing means of identification, the individuals who issue them, and the technologies used would be substantially improved.

Driver's Licenses: Still the Weakest Link in a Weak Chain

Driver's licenses and other state-issued identification cards are, by far, the most common means of identification used in the United States; therefore, these documents deserve special attention. Driver's licenses and state-issued identification cards are classic examples of multipurposive means of identification. The vast majority of Americans over sixteen years of age possess driver's licenses, and driver's licenses are one of the few identification documents that are widely accepted (others, such as passports or military IDs, are held by much smaller segments of the population). When boarding a plane, cashing a check, purchasing alcohol, or conducting similar activities, millions of Americans are asked to show ID. When asked for identification, most Americans present a driver's license; however, it was not created for this purpose and its reliability level does not meet that needed for the security uses for which it is commonly employed.

Problems with the Driver's License System

Prior to September 11, 2001, it was very easy to obtain driver's licenses in the United States using false or counterfeit documents, although it was a bit more difficult in some states than in others. One could even readily purchase a counterfeit driver's license on the street or on the Internet. Terrorists took advantage of these weak documents. Seven of the hijackers obtained Virginia driver's licenses by submitting false information to prove residency in the Commonwealth. The hijackers (and surely many others) took advantage of the fact that proof of residency could be obtained through a notarized affidavit of another Virginia resident. According to Paul J. McNulty, U.S. Attorney for the Eastern District of Virginia, two of the hijackers paid an illegal immigrant $100 to vouch for their residency.[29]

True, some loopholes have been closed in the wake of the terrorist attack (e.g., in Virginia, notarized affidavits were taken off the list of documents people can use to prove residency; in Florida, Governor Jeb Bush ordered that driver's licenses for foreigners must expire at the same time as their visas), but false driver's licenses can still be obtained easily. Between July 2002 and May 2003, the GAO's OSI agents conducted security tests in seven states and the District of Columbia to determine whether state motor vehicle agencies will issue driver's licenses to applicants who present counterfeit "breeder" documents,[30] such as counterfeit birth certificates, driver's licenses, and Social Security cards. As with the other GAO investigations, undercover OSI agents created fictitious identities and counterfeit documents using off-the-counter computers, printers, and software. The investigation found that Department of Motor Vehicle (DMV) officials generally did not recognize that the documents they were presented with were counterfeit. Therefore, DMV officials issued driver's licenses to the inspectors using the fictitious identifying information on the counterfeit breeder documents. In instances where DMV officials noted irregularities in the counterfeit documents, they still issued driver's licenses to the undercover agent and returned the counterfeit documents to him or her.[31]

Additionally, there are still people ready and willing to sell stolen or fake Social Security numbers and counterfeit birth certificates that can be used to obtain false or counterfeit driver's licenses. In August 2003, it was reported that phony ID cards, including Social Security cards and driver's licenses, still could be purchased in Washington, D.C., for anywhere between $20 and $135.[32] The low cost suggests that these IDs are readily available.

Efforts to make identification more reliable in the short run are most likely to involve driver's licenses and state-issued identification cards, and thus motor vehicle agencies. There is no sense in ignoring that driver's licenses and state-issued identification cards are widely used for homeland protection. Therefore, it is important to identify the weaknesses in the current identification system. (In a later section, I point to ways to improve driver's licenses and state-issued identification cards.) Weaknesses are found in three areas:

1. Processes
   - Fraudulent breeder documents (e.g., birth certificates, Social Security cards, baptismal records, etc.) often pass for the real thing. The wide availability of sophisticated graphic software programs and high-quality colored printers, as well as how-to books, make it easy to create counterfeit breeder documents.[33]
   - A state that issues a driver's license based on counterfeit breeder documents threatens the reliability of the entire system because driver's licenses issued in one state are honored by all others. Wrongdoers seek out states with the weakest protections against false identification.
   - States accept different documents to verify the identity and residency of the person applying for a driver's license or state-issued identification card, and some states only require proof of identity. The acceptable documents may include utility bills, birth certificates, voter registration cards, notarized statements, Social Security cards, health insurance cards, hunting licenses, and school IDs. The varying state requirements create an environment in which people who seek to obtain false IDs seek out the state with the most lax requirements.
   - States have differing rules about the issuance of driver's licenses or state-issued identification cards to foreign visitors. Some states tie the expiration date of the foreign visitor's driver's license to his or her visa expiration date, while other states allow the expiration date of the foreigner's driver's license to expire at the same interval as a citizen's driver's license.

- Each state issues its own driver's licenses and there are no standard minimum requirements. For instance, some states place the driver's photo on the left side of the card; other states place the photo on the right side of the card. States also use a wide range of authentication features, including holograms, bar codes, multiple photos, and magnetic strips. With these differences, Transportation Security Administration (TSA) personnel, police, retail clerks, and bartenders in one state may not know what a license in the other forty-nine states looks like, nor how reliable an out-of-state license is when they are presented with one.
- Some people hold multiple driver's licenses and state-issued identification cards. This threatens the integrity of the driver's license system and the idea that each person is limited to possessing one driver's license at a given time.

2. Personnel
   - Some employees at motor vehicle agencies have been easily bribed into issuing false driver's licenses.[34]
   - It is often difficult for the personnel issuing driver's licenses to identify counterfeit or false breeder documents, as the GAO's recent investigation notes.[35]
   - State motor vehicle agency personnel often do not follow security procedures and are not always alert to the possibility of fraud, as the GAO's recent investigation notes.[36]

3. Technology
   - Many of the identifying features currently used in driver's licenses are not the most reliable. For instance, a person's eye color can be altered through the use of contact lenses, and weight often varies from what is listed on the card.
   - Many driver's licenses are easy to tamper with or forge. As with breeder documents, the wide availability of sophisticated graphic software programs and high-quality colored printers, as well as how-to books, make it easy to create counterfeit IDs.[37]

The Internet: A Complicating Factor

The increasingly widespread use of the Internet to obtain false identification materials also poses problems for reliable means of identification, especially driver's licenses. David C. Myers, coordinator of the Fraudulent Identification Investigation Program for the Florida Division of Alcoholic Beverages and Tobacco, reported to the Senate in May 2000 that "about 30 percent of the false identification cards I see come from the Internet" and that "some false ID sites have received over 10,000 inquiries on a single day."[38] This is not that surprising, given that Myers also testified that many high-quality ID cards can be purchased on the Internet for anywhere between $30 and $300.[39] Thus, many underage college students, and certainly individuals with more nefarious plans, look to websites such as www.fakeidman.org and www.myoids.com to help them obtain fake IDs.

On the federal level it is illegal to produce knowingly or transfer without authority an identification document, authentication feature, or false identification document. It is also illegal for an individual to possess knowingly the aforementioned documents and features with the intent of defrauding the United States and to possess knowingly stolen or illegally produced documents.[40] Many states also have similar laws making it illegal to produce, possess, or transfer counterfeit or false state-issued identification cards and driver's licenses. While the law may seem basically clear on this issue, it is not so clear when it comes to prosecution. In his May 2002 testimony before the Senate, James G. Huse, inspector general of the SSA, clearly explained the problem prosecutors face when they find Social Security cards for sale on the Internet:

> [I]t is a felony under the Social Security Act to buy or sell a card that "purports to be" a Social Security card issued by the Commissioner. As you know, however, the cards sold over the Internet often carry easily removable stickers identifying them as "novelties." The difficulty in establishing fraudulent intent on the part of buyers or sellers makes prosecution of these cases problematic.[41]
>
> Many websites selling driver's licenses also have "novelty use" disclaimers.[42]

David C. Myers of the Florida Division of Alcoholic Beverages and Tobacco also noted in his May 2000 testimony before the Senate that it is difficult for state and local law enforcement agencies to take action against websites that sell IDs because it is difficult to locate their whereabouts and many operate outside the United States. He went on to testify: "Assistance from Federal agencies is very difficult. Very few agents, even on the state and federal levels, have any training in the area of counterfeit identification."[43] And while Mr. Myers has been successful in shutting down some websites, often—due to the nature of the Internet— the websites can reappear the next day with a new name.

More recently, in September 2003, John S. Pistole, Acting Assistant Director of the FBI's Counterterrorism Division, discussed the pervasiveness of false means of identification. In his testimony before the Senate, he said that it is not that false means of identification are new to law enforcement, but rather that the pervasiveness of the false means is new. The Internet and our technological sophistication—especially in terms of computer programs and printers—have made it so easy to produce high quality documents that "nearly anyone can be an expert."[44] Pistole also pointed out: "The tremendous growth of the Internet, the accessibility it provides to such an immense audience coupled with the anonymity it allows result in otherwise traditional fraud schemes becoming magnified when the Internet is utilized as part of the scheme."[45]

These few observations, and there are many others like them, convincingly show that the increasingly wide use of the Internet to obtain false means of identification poses problems for making means of identification more reliable.

Remedial Action

Some of the following recommendations address ways to make means of identification more reliable in the short term, while others will make them more reliable in the long term. *It is essential to develop reliable means of identification that work both online and offline.* The separation of "cards" and electronic means of identification is an artificial and short run policy. A person should be able to identify oneself online (say when ordering an airline ticket or a hotel room on the top floor of the Hay-Adams Hotel in Washington, D.C., which overlooks the White House) just as readily as one does at an airline counter or hotel desk. "Readers" of future means of identification should be able to verify the identity of a person with equal ease whether the person is physically present or thousands of miles away, connected by the Internet. Leading credit card and technology companies are developing a way for consumers to use their fingerprints in place of credit cards and cash. See Kelvin Maney, "Will that be Cash, Fingerprint or Cell Phone?" *USA Today*, 16 November 2003.

The government has undertaken some measures to improve the ways it operates in the online world and how it identifies people. For instance, the U.S. Postal Service has announced an In-Person Proofing system that can be used by government organizations and certificate authorities to allow them to communicate electronically with the Post Office in the future. To participate, an online application must be completed and the individual's identity and address must be verified online. Once that is done, the individual prints out the required form and takes it to the post office to complete the In-Person Proofing. Once this is successfully finished, the individuals can download the digital certificate.[46]

Another initiative the government is pursuing is E-Authentication, which is intended to serve and make government more responsive to citizens, businesses, government, and internal operations by establishing a common authentication service and infrastructure throughout the government.[47] The White House views this program as "develop[ing] a government-wide standard for identity verification online."[48] As discussed in drafts released for comment in the summer of 2003, E-Authentication will focus both on identity authentication (verifying that a person is who he claims to be) and attribute authentication (that the person is a member of a specific group, e.g., the military). The government has developed various levels of assurance for the initiative. These levels of assurance (minimal, low, substantial, and high) correspond with how certain the government is that the person is who he claims to be and what the risks are if the person is not who he claims to be.[49] Also as part of the E-Authentication initiative, the new Federal Identity and Credentialing Committee (FICC) is working to "simplify and unify authentication for federal employees" and to "create requirements for physical credentials, electronic credentials, and issuance."[50] These programs are small steps along the way to help improve the means of identification used in the online world, but much more remains to be done.

From all the suggestions and recommendations that a few of my colleagues on the Markle Task Force asked not to be included in our final report, I regret most the omission of the preceding point on the need for identification to work both online and offline. Their concern for privacy protection, which I agree is more serious online than offline, needs to be and can be addressed, but I am confident that the future will entail an ever greater "merger" of the online and offline worlds. Just as we seamlessly order movie tickets online or purchase them at the ticket counter, get doctors' prescriptions in person or have them e-mailed to pharmacies, so we will develop other systems, many of which will entail identification, to enable us to move readily from one realm to the other. Introducing a much higher level of security in one but not the other will greatly undermine security because it will invite those who seek to attack us to focus on the less covered front.

Governmental Remedies

There are numerous possible approaches from which to choose. This section flags two approaches: one that uses less sophisticated technology but is closer at hand, the other that is technologically more sophisticated but its implementation will be more difficult.

For governmental remedies, I focus on a three-phase process toward making more reliable means of identification. The first phase focuses on how the federal government can assist in making state driver's licenses and state-issued identification cards more reliable as quickly as possible because they are the most widely used form of identification in the

United States. The second phase focuses on adding the use of biometric and cryptographic technologies to various physical documents, such as driver's licenses and passports. The third phase deals with using "pure" biometrics.

All such developments should also address ways to balance our need to have more reliable means of identification with important concerns about privacy and civil liberties, especially concerns about how the data are stored and who may have access to the biometric data and for what purposes.

Phase One: Fortify Driver's Licenses. The federal government should conduct research on affordable methods of improving identification systems and making the entire identification mechanism more reliable. The government should encourage states to improve the system by adopting interstate standards and implementing them through the use of grants.

Many people do not view possession of counterfeit or false identification as a serious crime. For many college students, obtaining and using a fake ID is just another part of the college experience. Also, in each jurisdiction, the fines and penalties for individuals who possess, attempt to obtain, or sell counterfeit or false identification should be increased, as should the fines and penalties for individuals who knowingly supply such identification or knowingly allow people with such false or counterfeit means of identification to enter controlled areas. To combat the explosive growth of false identification on the Internet, federal authorities—in particular, the Secret Service, which enforces laws involving counterfeit and fraudulent identification—should be given resources to shut down websites that issue false or counterfeit IDs. Furthermore, Congress should pass legislation that would require servers to collaborate in tracing and shutting down websites that issue fraudulent or counterfeit identification.

The GAO's September 2003 report on the ability of undercover agents to obtain genuine driver's licenses using counterfeit documents highlights the problems with breeder documents.[51] Birth certificates are particularly problematic because they are issued by numerous jurisdictions and vary widely in format. Documents should be standardized. This will make it easier for DMV officials, and other officials who issue means of identification (such as passports) to recognize counterfeit documents. I also recognize the argument that standardization of the documents may make breeder documents easier to fake in the long run. For this reason, birth and death certificate records should be digitized and searchable for all states. This would allow DMV and other officials, such as Department of State officials who issue passports, to access birth and death certificate records electronically and it could resolve questions concerning the authenticity of these documents.

The data banks in which such information is stored should have privacy protection measures in place that address issues such as who can gain access to the data and for what purposes, as well as have enforcement policies. For instance, to protect civil liberties, audit trails should be established.

Only some states have made progress in making birth and death certificate records electronic. The good news is that the federal government is taking an initiative in this area; the bad news is that the initiative is still in its early stages. The federal initiative, called E-Vital, is establishing a common process through which birth and death record information can be analyzed, processed, collected, and verified.[52] This initiative will create a federal information repository of birth and death certificate records that will be electronically searchable. Because deaths will be certified online, this initiative will greatly decrease the amount of time it takes for a person's death to be officially reported to the SSA. To proceed, both institutional and financial hurdles must be overcome. Marsha Rydstrom, the SSA's project manager for E-Vital, said that the program faces problems with states that are not used to being told how to manage their data as well as potential funding problems, because the program's costs could range between $500,000 and $5 million in each state, depending on preexisting e-government capabilities.[53] Congress should fully fund the E-Vital program once initial testing of the program is complete.

Digitized birth and death certificate records will greatly help the following program, although this program should not be stalled in the states until E-Vital is fully operational. An elementary step in enhancing the validity of driver's licenses is to verify that the Social Security number a person presents when applying for a license is not someone else's. State motor vehicle agencies are supposed to collect Social Security numbers from driver's license and state-issued identification card applicants.[54] Motor vehicle agencies are allowed, but not required, to access the SSA's online database to verify the identity of the applicant. Prior to September 11, 2001, only twelve states used the Social Security Online Verification System (SSOLV) to verify the authenticity of Social Security numbers submitted to DMV agencies.[55] States may choose to verify the authenticity of the driver's license applicant's Social Security number in two ways: first in real time through an online check and second through batch checks in which multiple checks are performed and reported at a later time, generally within twenty-four to forty-eight hours.[56]

In 2004, the Institute for Communitarian Policy Studies conducted a survey of state motor vehicle departments (including the District of Columbia)[57] in an effort to track their progress in shoring up their driver's license issuance practices following the September 11 terrorist attacks. The survey culled information from a variety of sources and then asked that each DMV confirm or correct the information to reflect their most recent developments. Due to the changing nature of these statistics, the figures from the study may be subject to error for those DMVs that either did not respond to the survey or changed their procedures after the survey was conducted. (Henceforth, the study will be referred to as the "Institute survey.") According to the survey, sixteen states still do not take advantage of SSOLV.

One of the reasons the GAO notes for why states do not use SSOLV is the cost.[58] Because states are strapped for funds and the verifications would require additional time, money, and work, the U.S. Department of Transportation should provide the needed funds so that states will be encouraged to undertake this verification step.

When issuing driver's licenses, states accept various documents to prove both identity and residency, although some states do not require proof of residency. In general, states require at least one form of primary identification (e.g., a birth certificate or a previously issued driver's license). The second form of identification can often be from a list of documents that tend to be even less reliable than the primary identification. In some states they include health insurance cards, fishing licenses, gun permits, high school diplomas, and student ID cards. Persons with dubious intentions often look for the state with the weakest requirements. The American Association of Motor Vehicle Administrators (AAMVA) has taken a lead in this area by developing a list of acceptable, verifiable documents for state motor vehicle agencies to use. Congress should pass legislation requiring state motor vehicle agencies to only accept approved documents to prove identity and residency.

Similarly, states have varying rules for issuing driver's licenses to noncitizens in the United States. Some tie the driver's license's expiration date to the expiration date of the foreign visitor's visa, while others use the same interval as that used for U.S. citizens. Federal legislation should tie the expiration date of the driver's license or state-issued identification card to the expiration date of the foreign visitor's visa, as some states have already done.[59] (The Institute survey found that only twelve states take this step.)

The driver's license system presumes that one person holds one license at any given time. Unfortunately, as it stands now, state DMV agencies are unable to query other state DMV databases to make sure that a driver's license applicant does not already hold a license in another state and is not acknowledging that in his or her current attempt to obtain a license. The way to combat this problem is by integrating state motor vehicle databases for ordinary drivers. (The integration of databases has already been undertaken for those who hold commercial driver's licenses. The program, called the Commercial Driver's License Information System [CDLIS], was designed to make sure that commercial drivers only possess one driver's license and do not simultaneously carry licenses from more than one state. The program, mandated by the Commercial Vehicle Safety Act of 1986, has been in effect since 1992 and it has kept 871,000 individuals from obtaining licenses, according to the AAMVA.[60])

Currently, the only such database of noncommercial drivers available to state DMV officials is the National Driver Register (NDR), which employs the Problem Driver Pointer System (PDPS) to determine whether an applicant has had his driving privileges revoked by another state. This database does not, however, allow access to any information on applicants who have not had action taken against their licenses. As a result, there is no mechanism to prevent a person with a clean driving record (or someone who uses multiple names) from acquiring multiple licenses and ID cards from any number of states. Congress should mandate a program, similar to the Commercial Driver's License Information System, for all driver's license holders to ensure that an individual only holds one license from one state at a given time.

Driver's licenses vary greatly from state to state. Some states, such as Massachusetts, place multiple pictures on driver's licenses—a large picture and a smaller version of the picture. In some states, such as Virginia, the picture appears on the left side of the license, while in other states, such as Oklahoma, the picture is located on the right side. Some states use a single barcode on their licenses (e.g., New York); other states use multiple barcodes (e.g., Virginia); and some licenses still in circulation do not even have barcodes (e.g., Oklahoma licenses issued prior to September 2003). The same is true for holograms. For these reasons, it is often difficult for TSA personnel, police, and retail clerks in one state to know what valid licenses in the other forty-nine states look like. State driver's licenses and identification cards should meet minimum uniform standards concerning the data content and the verifiability of the credential. Although all states must adopt these standards, there can still be room for variations among the states, say placing a state seal or motto on the license. These uniform standards can also deal with problems about the ease with which driver's licenses can be tampered with or forged. Also, the card's electronic code—magnetic strips, smart chips, whatever the uniform mean may be—should be encrypted and should contain all the information already on the driver's license.

As the GAO recently noted in its report on the use of counterfeit documents to obtain genuine licenses, many DMV officials do not recognize counterfeit documents when these are presented to them.[61] State motor vehicle agencies should provide their employees with ongoing, detailed training about how to spot counterfeit or false documents and they should provide law enforcement personnel with guidelines for how to check the validity of driver's licenses. Periodically, a state could conduct spot checks to see whether officials spot the false documents and whether they follow protocol in those instances. For example, in states that require DMV officials to confiscate documents they believe are counterfeit or false, are officials complying with these guidelines? To better meet these responsibilities, *state motor vehicle agencies should launch aggressive oversight, auditing, and anti-corruption policies to help prevent fraud and make it easier to detect it when it occurs in the driver's license issuing process.* Certainly, DMV officials also need to receive detailed training on how to spot counterfeit breeder documents.

Phase Two: Add Biometrics. Biometric data already exists on driver's licenses and for years biometric data has been used to link an individual to an identification card. For instance, driver's licenses include a photo as well as other identifying information, such as the height, weight, and eye color of the driver. Unfortunately, these biometrics are not the most reliable. Individuals can gain or lose weight (or lie about it) and eye color can be easily changed using contact lenses. Furthermore, the photo may not resemble the driver's license holder very well as the cardholder's appearance may change over the period of time his license is valid (e.g., he could change hair styles, his hair could gray or be colored, or he could lose hair). The addition of new forms of biometric data on driver's licenses, data that are more difficult to change and are more specific to the individual, can further assist our ability to more reliably and accurately verify an individual's identity when additional levels of security are needed, for instance at airports.

(In such an instance, if fingerprint data are used on driver's licenses, the passenger could place one finger on a scanner and his fingerprint could be compared against the one on the driver's license to see whether the passenger is who he claims to be.) Furthermore, because these biometric data are much more specific to an individual than the current biometric data in use, it will become exceptionally difficult—and some say nearly impossible—for an individual to switch his or her identity once identity is established.[62] Therefore, the second phase of making means of identification reliable should focus on studying how biometric and cryptographic technologies can be used to make driver's licenses more reliable. Currently, seventeen states are either collecting or planing to collect some form of biometric information from their residents, according to the Institute survey.

One reason why the addition of advanced biometrics to driver's licenses might be postponed is that the introduction of many new forms of biometrics would require the introduction of "readers" in more than a million locations. The good news is that the technology for reading biometric data is improving rapidly (especially in terms of re-liability, cost, and convenience), so much so that, over the next several years, many handheld devices and personal computers will come with built-in fingerprint readers that can prevent someone who steals such a device from gaining access to its data.[63] Another reason the addition of biometrics to driver's licenses may take some time is the large size of the population—more than 200 million people have driver's licenses and state-issued ID cards.[64] Thus, even small error rates in the tech-nology could have significant effects, given the size of the population. Still, biometrics stand to pose a great benefit to making means of identification more reliable and they deserve further study and, when possible, implementation.

There are a wide variety of options from which policy makers may choose. Among the biometric options are iris scans, fingerprint recognition, facial recognition, hand geometry, retina scans, signature recognition, and voice recognition.[65] For example, iris scans involve an individual placing his or her eye close to a reader that identifies the unique characteristics of the individual's iris. The reader, a camera, captures a high-resolution image of the iris. To date, iris scans have been employed in special fast-track lanes at Schiphol Airport in Amsterdam. The iris scan program allows participants to move through security quickly. Fingerprint recognition technology captures a person's unique fingerprint from impressions made by the ridges in the finger. The image is recorded by a scanner, enhanced, and then converted into a template. Systems that utilize fingerprints sometimes compare an individual's fingerprint directly against a database. For instance, the FBI maintains a database full of fingerprints, called the Integrated Automated Fingerprint Identification System, which contains about 45 million prints and is used in the agency's investigations.[66] Other times, a person's fingerprint is compared against the biometric data stored on the card. For instance, immigration officials have begun matching an individual at the U.S. border with the fingerprint stored on his or her ID card that was issued by the Department of State or the former INS in the last five years.[67] Facial recognition technology identifies people by analyzing facial features that are not easily altered. Cameras in London use facial recognition technology to identify criminals; and more recently, the Illinois Department of Motor Vehicles has employed the technology in its driver's licensing system to prevent individuals from obtaining multiple driver's licenses.[68] To place the biometric data on driver's licenses, policy makers may choose from magnetic strips, two-dimensional bar codes, laser cards, and smart cards.[69] Many cards that use the aforementioned types of biometric data are examining the use of smart cards because they can store data and be used for multiple purposes, as well as because each card has its own encryption system.[70]

Phase Three: "Pure" Biometrics. Biometric technology is promising; yet because it is still relatively futuristic, its treatment in this section will be brief. There is little doubt that in the long run—some measure it in years, others believe it will take longer—biometric data will provide a reliable means of identification and there will be no need to carry physical cards. One's finger, face, iris, or some other unique feature will provide all the identification one needs. Therefore, the introduction of a pure biometric system should also be examined. It is best to proceed on two levels: (1) meta-analysis, overview, and codification of what is known, the result of various ongoing studies in the private sector and in the government; and (2) the issuance of RFPs to invite additional studies to cover well-known lacunas or those lacunas the said summaries of state-of-the-art would reveal.

The biggest concern among critics of biometric technology is that this information could give the government too much access to personal data about American citizens. Mark Rotenberg of the Electronic Privacy Information Center refers to biometrics as "the digital equivalent of allowing police to go through your home without a warrant."[71] And while this criticism is not consistent with the facts, all such studies of biometrics should also address ways to balance our need to have more reliable means of identification with important concerns about privacy and civil liberties. Among the privacy issues that should be addressed are how biometric data should be stored, who should be able to have access to and use the data, and what possible, unintended consequences may result from data collection.

Private Sector Remedies

The private sector has shown repeatedly that it can and does create successful means of identification. For instance, many corporations are devising their own purposive means of identification, some of which are low-tech while others are high-tech. And some companies will not even allow an employee to enter the premises if he or she has forgotten the company-issued ID, even if the employee can present a driver's license to security officials.[72] In other words, the private sector is also working to develop more reliable means of identification on its own. ATM cards are a case in point. This section examines whether the private sector could produce more reliable means of identification, make them widely acceptable by providing incentives for people to use them, and thus ease the obstacles currently faced both in terms of convincing people that such means of identification will not be overly intrusive and that the means of identification can help security.

Given the reluctance to embrace stronger means of identification issued by governmental authorities, even if these means are merely issued by the states and are not required to be on the person or presented upon demand, and given the general trend in the public sector (including agencies such as the Department of Defense and the CIA) toward relying on the private sector, I examine whether the private sector could produce more reliable means of identification, make them widely acceptable by providing incentives for people to use them, and thus ease the obstacles currently faced both in terms of convincing people that such means of identification will not be intrusive and that the means of identification can help security. One may even suggest that driver's licenses should be subcontracted to private companies, just as many other parts of our military and intelligence work are subcontracted to profit-making corporations.

No one in the private sector, so far, has come forward with exactly what is needed to make our means of identification more reliable, but there are several indications that there are major corporations and industry groups that might well be interested in helping the government in this way. For instance, shortly after the terrorist attack in September 2001, Oracle CEO Larry Ellison suggested making government databases more effective by consolidating them and making identification cards, such as driver's licenses and Social Security cards, more secure with digital technology (like that used on credit cards or smart cards). He offered to provide the government with the needed software for free; and in the summer of 2002, he reiterated his offer.[73]

The notion that the private sector can provide more reliable means of identification is also supported by a Foundation for the Defense of Democracies publication by Eli Lehrer. Lehrer favors the adoption of a market-based national identity system. Under his proposal, the government would set standards for the system, but the private sector would run the primarily voluntary biometric identification database (only convicted felons and non-citizen visitors would be required to register).[74]

Although it appears that the private sector is interested in having more reliable means of identification, the question remains: if people could purchase what I call high-security cards from various companies for, say, $65 to $100, and if the cards could serve people well in many different areas of their lives, including cashing checks, entering buildings, and standing in special, shorter lines in airports, could the card catch on? (This does presuppose that the government will be able to use the private sector's means of identification under some private/public partnership arrangement.) Would it ease the problems at hand? What incentives might be needed to encourage the private sector to develop such high-security cards?

Take just one example of where such cards might be used—at airports—and the incentives it could provide. Private-sector cards, like the one described above that more reliably identifies people, may be particularly appealing to frequent flyers who wish to pass through airport security more quickly. Such accelerated screening lanes already exist in some airports, including at Tel Aviv's Ben Gurion and Amsterdam's Schiphol Airports where biometric scans are used. Actually, the United States has a similar system in place for international travelers, called INSPASS. The program, which has some forty-five thousand active participants, relies on biometrics to accelerate immigration screening at large international airports, such as New York's John F. Kennedy and Washington's Dulles International, among others.[75] INSPASS's success in accelerating immigration screening and its acceptance by many frequent travelers suggest that a card that can accelerate security screening at airports could be widely accepted and desired by travelers. This does not mean that individuals holding ID cards would not walk through metal detectors and place their items on a conveyor belt like everyone else, just that, on average, people who have the card would move through faster security lines.

Thus, if voluntary, private-sector cards could reliably identify individuals, then routine identification (not to be confused with entering highly-secured areas) could become more reliable with little to no cost to the government. Moreover, the stigma now attached to ID cards may well be reduced because people would voluntarily purchase the private-sector cards. In addition, private-sector cards could also be used for non-security purposes. If the private-sector card were a smart card embedded with a computer chip and encryption technology, then the card could also potentially be used as an ATM card or credit card.

The government should examine private-sector alternatives to making means of identification more reliable. The Department of Homeland Security should convene a panel of representatives from corporations to determine what incentives can encourage the private sector to market reliable cards that people would be free to purchase. Among the options to be examined is whether such cards could be used for fast tracks in airports, as well as for ATMs or other such purposeful uses. The application of systems that the private sector is developing to protect identities over distances, electronically, and for national security should also be examined.

Privacy and Accountability Protections

New measures that are introduced to enhance security and, more generally, law enforcement are often examined in terms of whether they are of merit in and of themselves. However, any benefits to the common good must be evaluated in terms of their potential threat to individuals' privacy. Therefore, civil libertarians' concerns about privacy should be addressed in all matters concerning more reliable means of identification. Studies of ways to make means of identification more reliable should include the quest for ways to balance our need to have more reliable means of identification with important concerns about privacy and civil liberties.

Most privacy concerns do not arise out of the improved identification per se, but rather out of the questions that concern the ways in which data about a person are collected, stored, and used. For instance, if a toll booth camera identifies a car as one that previously paid for a toll (by the use of EZ Pass, for example)—but immediately erases that information, then there would be fewer privacy concerns than if these data were stored and collected and then made available to government agencies and profit-making bodies. As Matt LeMieux of the ACLU argues, "Even if the government says that it will be used for only one purpose, there are plenty of examples in our nation's history—and Social Security is one of them—where the government went beyond the original intent."[76]

Indeed, a strong case can be made that to the *extent that data collection takes place at all, it should be made more reliable in order to protect people's privacy.* This is because when the authorities believe that names and addresses are unreliable, they will collect much more information in order to verify a person's identity (say, information about birthmarks, known associations, and so on).

A good identification system must have an expeditious correction mechanism in order to protect individual rights. Thus, if a person claims to have been misidentified and hence he or she is prevented from, say, flying, then he or she should be able to show as expeditiously as possible that a mistake has been made.

For personal data such as digitized birth and death certificate records, the owner of the data should have privacy protection measures in place that address issues such as who may have access to the data and for what purposes, as well as have enforcement policies. For instance, audit trails, which could detect unauthorized use of data and thus help deter it, should be established.

Aside from internal supervision, as well as oversight from Congress, the courts, and the DHS's Privacy Officer and Civil Rights and Liberties Officer, there should be a *Citizen's Accountability Board,* comprised of illustrious citizens who are not currently employed by the government or expect to be any time soon, say deans of law schools, possibly limited to those with security clearance. The board would release summary statements to the public. It would be best if this board would review whether the more reliable means of identification are being properly issued by government agencies, what the error rates in the system are, and how much time it takes to fix the errors.

Finally, the Department of Transportation or the Department of Homeland Security should issue regular progress reports so that the media and the public will be aware of the states that are cooperating with required programs and measures to make means of identification more reliable and, by implication, the public will be aware of states that are not cooperating.

Collateral Gains

If more reliable means of identification were available for national security purposes then a great number of other safety and nonsafety issues could be alleviated and collateral gains would be possible. This section examines gains that can be realized if means of identification are made more reliable.

Protecting the Innocent

A major source of the miscarriage of justice is the well-established and widely known fact that people are misidentified and jailed for crimes they did not commit. With more reliable means of identification, the incidents in which innocent people are detained, incarcerated, or barred from flying, driving, entering the United States, and obtaining security sensitive jobs should decrease. This alone is a major justification for the introduction of more reliable means of identification.

Identity Theft and Credit Card Fraud

The Federal Trade Commission (FTC) reported that it received more than 214,000 complaints of identity theft in 2003, up from 160,000 complaints in 2001 and 86,000 complaints in 2002.[77] These reported complaints are low-end estimates of the prevalence of identity theft. A September 2003 FTC survey estimated that within the past year 3.25 million Americans discovered that their personal information had been misused.[79]

By stealing identifying information from other individuals or by creating fictitious identifiers, individuals can obtain numerous credit card accounts and often charge exorbitant amounts of money for luxury vacations, electronics, and other high-end items, as well as use that information to obtain other types of credit, such as car loans. To show how big a problem this has become, one need only look at the FTC's most recent estimate that the total annual cost to identity theft victims is about $5 billion.[80] For individuals who have had their identities stolen and credit cards opened in their names, the fight against credit card fraud is an uphill battle. For young people, the fraud can be particularly devastating, preventing them from getting the credit they need to get started in life; and for seniors it is a disruption that causes undue stress and financial problems during their golden years. Credit card fraud can also harm homeland security as terrorists may use credit cards from unsuspecting Americans to help finance their operations. If means of identification were more reliable, then such fraud could be more difficult to commit and easier to detect.

Voter Fraud

Identification difficulties lead to voter fraud. In many states, deceased voters remain on the voting rolls and individuals with false or counterfeit identification can vote in person or often request absentee ballots; other times, picture identification is not required. If means of identification were more reliable, then voter fraud could be easier to detect.

Fugitives

While the exact number of felons at large is not available, some estimates have been made: in 2002 the FBI said it looks for about 12,000 fugitives at any one time.[81] The lack of a reliable means of identification makes it difficult for law enforcement officials to catch fugitives who have skipped court appearances or those who have warrants out for their arrest. When a police officer pulls over a speeding driver in Oregon and checks his driver's license, the officer will be unable to determine that the man pulled over for speeding has a warrant out for his arrest in Tennessee if the speeder is using a false or counterfeit ID. If means of identification were more reliable, law enforcement would better be able to reliably identify the speeder. Likewise, more reliable means of identification would help identify individuals who are prohibited from driving after several DUI convictions, but still get behind the wheel of a car.

Employment

Convicted sexual predators often depart the jurisdiction of their offense, later applying for jobs at child care centers and schools elsewhere in the nation. While their names may be compiled in a national network, such a database is useless if the predator has a counterfeit or false means of identification. In much the same way, abusive healthcare workers—particularly those taking care of the elderly—often apply for jobs taking care of the vulnerable even after having been previously caught and their employment terminated. Efforts to warn other healthcare providers will be more successful with more reliable means of identification.

Other Programs

The lack of reliable identification can pose great costs to government programs such as student loan, affordable housing, and food stamp programs, and it causes a loss of revenue in terms of individual income tax payments.

Conclusion

The old cliché that a chain is only as strong as its weakest link applies to the issue at hand. "No-fly" lists, passenger profiling systems, and scores of other security systems are greatly weakened if people can readily obtain false or counterfeit IDs. Improving means of identification requires not only new and better technologies (especially biometrics and cryptography), but also training and supervision of those who issue IDs, and proper processes to validate the identities that are being certified.

Reference is not to a national ID card but rather to the means of identification that people use when they seek to enter an area to which access is legitimately limited, whether it is a military base, an airplane, or even the United States. Therefore, while it is undesirable for an individual to have to keep on their person at all times a mandatory national ID card, the government should offer incentives for citizens to voluntarily purchase special IDs designed to expedite entry into controlled areas, such as airports. All such changes in means of identification must be carefully scrutinized to ensure that they will not violate privacy and other individual rights. Here too, processes (e.g., audit trails), personnel (e.g., citizen review boards and improved personnel training), and technologies (e.g., biometrics and cryptography) can be of great service. All in all, we see here one more case in which we need to work out a carefully crafted balance between security and rights.

Author Note: This chapter has a special history. In 2002 and 2003, I participated in the Task Force on National Security in the Information Age convened by the Markle Foundation. It resulted in two reports of considerable interest. The first is the Markle Foundation Task Force, *Protecting America's Freedom in the Information Age* (New York: Markle Foundation, October 2002). The second is the Markle Foundation Task Force, *Creating a Trusted Network for Homeland Security* (New York: Markle Foundation, December 2003). (Both reports are available at http://www.markletaskforce.org.) The second followed a suggestion that I made to the co-chairs of the Task Force, Zoë Baird and James L. Barksdale, that they authorize the creation of a subgroup to study the issues discussed in this chapter. The subgroup on Reliable Identification for Homeland Protection and Collateral Gains was formed and I served as its chair. Its members included Robert D. Atkinson, Stewart

A. Baker, Eric Benhamou, William P. Crowell, David Farber, Mary McKinley, Paul Rosenzweig, Jeffrey Smith, James B. Steinberg, Paul Schott Stevens, and Michael Vatis. Following consultations with the members of the task force—especially William P. Crowell, Michael Vatis, and Robert D. Atkinson—I drafted and redrafted the paper several times. The final report (December 2003) varied considerably from what I would have written on my own. Hence, this chapter draws on the report of the sub-group, although it differs from it substantially and includes more recent data. I am indebted to the members of the task force for their comments and above all to Deirdre Mead for excellent research assistance.

6
THE LIMITS OF NATION BUILDING

One of the great clichés of our time is that one can and should "drain" the swamp in which terrorists breed by both democratizing and developing the economies of countries such as Afghanistan and Iraq. An important part of the thesis that the best way to shore up national security—while protecting if not advancing the elements of a free society—is the neo-Wilsonian idea of changing the regimes of other countries, nation building in general, and democratization in particular. As I see it, foreign powers can rarely accomplish nation building—however that is defined—and it tends to be costly, not merely in economic resources and political capital, but also in human lives. Hence, for both empirical, social science considerations, and normative ones, foreign powers had best greatly scale back their ambitions and promises. The more these powers focus whatever resources they are willing and able to commit for the intervention at hand on a modest agenda, the more good they will do for the nation they seek to help and for themselves.

There are many reasons why superpowers and other powers are tempted to promise nation building. They believe in the value of forging nations and helping their development. They are keen to share with others that which they hold dear—domestic peace, the blessing of democratic politics, and the rich fruits of developed economies. They believe in the possibility of human progress and have a weakness for positive thinking, which leads them to hold that such developments can be brought about relatively easily, especially if one is dedicated to espousing them. They also follow a practice common in domestic politics—launching programs with great fanfare, which dazzles the media, the voters, and sometimes the legislature. Often, these same groups do not pay much mind to the complicated details of what can actually be done and achieved. Thus, politicians can promise cake and they do not have to deliver it—for instance, the five-year, $15-billion plan that the United States promised to fight HIV/AIDS globally. And if governments' feet are held to the fire, they often claim to have made good on their promises by defining down what is considered nation building, democratization, or economic reconstruction. Mission accomplished—by public relations.

In contrast, I advocate a foreign policy that recognizes that one size does not fit all; that unmodified Western ways may well not be suitable for other cultures and societies; that making progress happen via long distances, in other people's countries, is very taxing; that positive thinking is just that—positive thinking, which cannot deliver the mail, and certainly not move mountains; and above all, that a greatly scaled-back, restrained agenda ensures credibility, making future achievements somewhat more feasible.

A Three-Legged Definition

Defining nation building should no longer be deferred. Unfortunately, there is no social science or intellectual academy where terminology is clearly defined and its consistent use enforced. The term "nation building" is generally used to describe three different but related tasks: unification of disparate ethnic groups, democratization, and economic reconstruction.

In its original usage, nation building was frequently identified with unifying diverse ethnic groups within a state; that is, community building: "A major object of nation-building was to weld the disparate elements of the populace into a congruent whole by forging new identities at the national (state) level at the expense of localism and particularistic identities."[1] Creating a sense of national identity was seen to be important for the formation of the state itself. Nation building means "both the formation and establishment of the new state itself as a political entity and the processes of creating viable degrees of unity, adaptation, achievement, and a sense of national identity among the people."[2]

Another view of nation building emphasizes improvements in governance.[3] Creating effective governance means implementing the rule of law, battling corruption, installing democracy, and ensuring freedom of the press.[4] Historically, nation building encompassed "an effort to construct a government that may or may not be democratic, but preferably is stable."[5] Today, nation building often "implies the attempt to create democratic and secure states."[6] This democratization imperative was particularly stressed during the presidencies of Ronald Reagan and Bill Clinton, both of whom sought the "enlargement" of democracy around the world.

A third view sees economic reconstruction as an important part of nation building. It is suggested that when the economy is improved, a more stable and better functioning state can evolve. Also, economic well-being is associated with democratization.[7] It is best not to equate, as many do, economic reconstruction with economic development. Economic reconstruction assumes that there was a well-functioning economy, but that some catastrophic event, such as a war or civil strife, undermined it and the economy must be put back on its feet. This sense of nation building was particularly employed with regard to the rebuilding of Japan and Germany after World War II. The term "economic development" is best reserved for building a modern economy where none previously existed, a much more demanding task.

Whether one uses the term "nation building" to refer to only one or more of these meanings (many use all three, interchangeably), one should take into account that the reference is to *nation*, not *state* building.

A nation is widely understood to be a community invested in a state.[8] It hence entails much more than merely forming a state, say by granting independence to a previous colony. It entails both forming a state and a community where none previously existed, or shoring up one that has not been firmly or properly constructed previously, or whose existence has been undermined, often by war or inner strife.

A state can exist without its citizens having the kind of loyalties that, in political matters, would give precedence to the state when it comes into conflicts with member groups such as tribes or ethnic groups. Such a layering of loyalties is essential if a nation is to stay together and avoid secessions or civil war, without relying merely or mainly on force.

Behind these statements is a bit of social and political theory that should be spelled out, especially the notion that a nation is more than a state, that it has strong elements of community, at least an imagined one. Commitments to the common good and to one another's community are essential because effective collective decision making often entails imposing on various participants sacrifices for the common good (e.g., to protect the environment for future generations). If these sacrifices are not backed up by shared values and bonds, the key elements of community, they will not be treated as legitimate, and hence will either have to be effected through force, or will not be effectively enforced. (This view contrasts with the notion that the state is largely a place where various interest groups meet, work out deals and contracts, and make exchanges. Therefore, no loyalties or commitments are needed, as self-interest provides the necessary glue.)[9]

My main thesis is that significantly advancing any of the elements of nation building, let alone all three of them, by external powers, is under most circumstances difficult to accomplish, and at best requires a considerable commitment of resources and time. Moreover, assiduously promoting these elements can be counterproductive.

Thus, my claim rests on both a general and a specific observation. The general observation is that *deliberate*, purposive societal change of any importance is difficult to achieve. For the discussion at hand

(and for many others), it is essential to distinguish deliberate and purposive societal change (sometimes referred to as social engineering), that is, societal changes that policy makers and public authorities seek to bring about (such as the war against drugs, poverty, cancer)—and societal change that occurs naturally, all on its own. (The difference is akin to the difference between a river that is changing its course naturally, which requires no effort, versus building and manning canals and locks to change its course, often at considerable cost.) Social engineering, in contrast to physical, is a very limited art, facing huge obstacles as it aims to change what human and social nature provided. In this sense, it is unnatural. Social engineering also raises numerous moral issues that greatly limit what can be done.

By and large, the record of major deliberate efforts to significantly change societies by public authorities have failed or achieved much less than was sought. All planned societies—including such major societies as the USSR and China—not only failed to achieve their various goals (abolish stratification, religion, the family, and the state), but their command and control systems imploded. The plans of social democracies to reallocate wealth in a significant manner have made limited progress. The Great Society goals in the United States remain largely unaccomplished. Major changes occurred in all these societies, but not as the result of public policies. Often, they reflected the work of spontaneously arising social movements (in the sense that they were neither initiated nor controlled by public authorities or even private corporations, nor were they predicable) who both made changes of their own and pushed the government into making changes. These included, in earlier eras, various religious movements; in the beginning of the 20th century, the progressive movement; and in its latter half, the civil rights, environmental, and women's movements, among others.

The reasons why significant, deliberate, purposive societal change is difficult to come by are numerous. To study them would require a major volume. Suffice it to say that they entail changing long-established personal predispositions, habits, and relationships that resist change unless those involved seek to modify them for their own reasons and, above all, motives. Such changes require reengineering deeply ingrained moral and social cultures and recasting societal structures, especially power relations and allocations of assets, which are particularly resilient.

The reasons why external powers are particularly hampered in promoting deliberate change are numerous. These include a limited understanding of the local culture and societal formation; an unwillingness to make the sacrifices involved; the opposition generated from the mere presence of outsiders; and faulty theories of societal engineering, especially the belief that change can be readily and quickly introduced at low human and economic costs. As Gary T. Dempsey writes:

> Nation building is perhaps the most intrusive form of foreign intervention there is. It is the massive foreign regulation of the policy making of another country. The process usually entails the replacement or, in the case of a country in a state of anarchy, the creation of governmental institutions and a domestic political leadership that are more to the liking of the power or powers conducting the intervention. Since such profound interference tends to elicit resistance, the nation-building process typically requires a substantial military presence to impose the nation-building plan on the target country.[10]

Western attempts to turn Iraq and Afghanistan into shining, prosperous democracies provide painful lessons in the grave limitations that even superpowers and their allies face when they engage in such large-scale social engineering. The focus on the formal features of democracy, such as elections and constitution writing, hardly conceals the fact that many of the foundations for anything that would even resemble a democratic form of government are missing in these nations. One needs only to be reminded that elections were also carried out in the USSR and in Saddam's Iraq and that now they take place in nations such as North Korea and Iran. Moreover, the USSR had one of the most liberal constitutions ever written. Many nations in South America copied the

American Constitution but were under the rule of one military junta or another for generations.

I turn next to show that this general observation applies with specific force to nation building by outsiders.

Historical Anti-Precedents: Nation Building–Breaking Away

Nation building has been successful on a large scale in earlier generations by working against and breaking away from superpower and external nations, rather than being guided by them or under their tutelage. The well-known period of wars of national liberation took place when scores of ethnic groups rebelled against colonial powers and gained their independence, often after prolonged bloodshed. Most nations that now make up Latin America, Africa, large segments of Asia, and the Balkans were formed in this way.

In other cases, nations were cobbled together from fragments, but again only after prolonged wars that gave voice to a fledgling community, rather than this voice being engendered by an external power. These famously include the formation of Germany, the United Kingdom, Italy, Chile, and the United States.

Moreover, in many of those cases where external powers did fashion a state they assumed would be a nation, the result was severe tensions among the ethnic groups that were combined into these "nations"—for instance, Burundi, Iraq, Nigeria, Somalia, and Rwanda. They were often held together only under the thumb of a tyrant and following much bloodshed. In other cases, these artificial constructions did not hold together, India and Yugoslavia, for instance.

In short, if by nation building one means cobbling together various fragments to make one community, then most nations were built *in opposition to* external powers rather than *by them*. And to the extent that these powers fashioned new states, they were born in blood, bathed in it, and rarely matured to be a nation, as the term is commonly understood.

Furthermore, such efforts have become more difficult in this age of mass political awareness and heightened antagonism to foreign power, as the USSR and the United States discovered in Afghanistan and the United States in Iraq, among many other examples.

The Limits of Democratization

The record of exporting democracy is not much better. A study conducted by the Carnegie Endowment for International Peace found that out of the eighteen forced regime changes to which American ground troops were committed, only five resulted in sustained democratic rule.[11] These countries include Germany, Japan, and Italy, in which conditions prevailed that are lacking elsewhere. The reasons for the exceptional success in these countries are explored below. Two other countries, listed as democratized, actually have yet to earn this title: Panama and Grenada.

The late Senator Daniel Patrick Moynihan used the phrase "defining deviancy down" to describe the practice of considering items of behavior as legitimate and legal that used to be considered deviant and illegal. One side effect of this practice is that public authorities can vastly improve the measurements of their achievements—without doing anything new or additional. Thus, crime statistics plunge—when whole categories of crimes are no longer viewed as illegal acts. A similar damaging tendency can be observed with regard to democracies. When it turns out that it is very difficult to export or even domestically construct a democratic polity under many conditions, various public policy makers keep the triumphant march of democracy going by declaring "done" for scores of nations that, at best, have only some democratic features. Elections are especially used for these sleight-of-hand democratizations, leading to what Max Boot, among others, has referred to as "one person, one vote, one time."[12] Others try to deal with this catch, by referring to "electoral democracies" to hint that they might not be regular nor full-fledged ones, but this hint escapes many. As a result, what normative power the title of "democracy" entails is lost when one can get it doing so little. Cynicism is fostered when countries labeled democratic are corrupt to the core, do not have a free press nor the rule of law, or only one political party, or a military that can veto whatever the legislature rules are labeled democratic. A democracy does not have to meet all the criteria, and there are differences in the political systems among those considered democracies, but defining the term down so far is neither good political science nor sound public policy. Max Boot termed South Africa a "flourishing democracy."[13] President Hu Jintao of China stated that China must "ensure that people can exercise democratic elections," yet his government does not tolerate a free press or an opposition party.[14] William Safire called Afghanistan after the fall of the Taliban a "creeping democracy," citing as an example the presence of "newly liberated women."[15] This is a surprising observation because numerous other reports suggest that women's status has barely changed. Afghanistan's court went ballistic when a woman sang on TV and the *New York Times* reported that young women set themselves on fire to escape the harsh realities of life in Afghanistan.[16]

The difficulties that the United States and its allies experienced in democratizing Afghanistan and Iraq are but the most recent examples in a long list of failures, which include Bosnia, Cambodia, Cuba, the Dominican Republic, Kosovo, Somalia, and South Vietnam. U.S. nation building attempts in Panama, Haiti, Nicaragua, and Cuba all took more than 10 years—Panama's engagement lasted 33 years; today, none of these countries can be considered a successful democracy.[17] As Thomas Carothers put it, "the idea that there's a small democracy inside every society waiting to be released just isn't true."[18]

There is no agreement as to what makes a democracy, although there are extensive and strong studies of the subject by such scholars as Graham Allison,[19] Archie Brown,[20] Thomas Carothers,[21] Robert A. Dahl,[22] and Adeed Dawisha and Karen Dawisha.[23] In addition, there is the extensive work and the publications of the National Endowment for Democracy, headed by Carl Gershman, which include an entire journal devoted to the subject at hand.[24]

Some scholars insist that each situation is unique and that only by immersing oneself in the particular history and culture of the country can one establish what must be done. By contrast, I agree with those scholars who suggest that a general theory of democracy formation is possible. As part of this approach, it seems beneficial to draw up a checklist of the factors that go into making a democracy. The list is best divided into *facilitating* factors and *constituting* factors. The first list gives the conditions that ease or hinder the formation of democracy. (They can also be referred to as the democratic infrastructure.) The listed factors are not all or even each "prerequisites," because substitutes might be found, but their presence clearly improves the probability that a democracy will be formed and sustained. The second list informs us as to what the needed building blocks are. Both lists can be used to indicate how ready a country is to be democratized and what, particularly, is missing.

Two methodological comments are called for at this juncture. The lists here provided are far from exhaustive and are merely provided as a first approximation. And one should keep in mind that there is an interaction effect among the various factors: namely, if one factor is available, it eases the formation of the others; but if one factor is maximized while all the others are grossly neglected, then these other factors are likely to retard democratization. More or less even development is superior to a tilted one.

Drawing on the works already cited, a few others, and my own observations, here are the two tentative lists. (All variables should be read as if preceded with the statement, "the more, the better," without concern that excessive levels could be reached, because these do not occur.)

Facilitating Factors

Facilitating factors include:

- Law and order, pacification
- Literacy, general education, civic education
- Economic development, separation of economic power from political power, leveling of economic differences
- A sizable, developed middle class

- The rule of law, independent judgments, respect for law enforcement authorities
- Civil society, voluntary associations, communities

Constituting Factors

Constituting factors include:

- Political leaders and parties have unencumbered ability to compete for support and votes
- The determination of criteria regarding eligibility for public office
- The assurance of free and fair elections
- Formulation of a constitutional order and process that ensures power-sharing as well as separation of power, essential for check and balance among the executive, legislative, and judicial branches
- A low level of corruption (high level of transparency)
- Protection of minority rights
- Freedom of association
- Freedom of expression
- Freedom of the press
- The enumeration of rights people have with respect to the government

To reiterate, these lists are but a preliminary attempt to outline the factors needed to form a sustainable democracy. They assist one another. Above all, they highlight how difficult it is to form a democracy where many of the factors are in short supply. Even a cursory examination of most of them suffices to note that developing them will be difficult, slow, costly, and, above all, next to impossible for outsiders to achieve. Cultivating respect for law where little exists, making a middle class, greatly reducing corruption where it is rampant, are all difficult tasks.

Economic "Reconstruction": From the Stone Age?

Arguably, economic reconstruction—if one means reconstruction rather than new development—may be the easiest (not easy) task for the three nation-building processes to achieve. If the country at issue had a relatively developed economy, was industrialized, had laws protecting private property, a solid banking system, a trained labor force, and so on—and if these were disrupted due to war or for some other reason—then these can be jump-started again with relative ease. The reasons are that self-interest will make people reopen their shops once they are free to do so, which in turn will create demand for products, and so on, all with relatively little planning or intervention. Outsiders can help in shoring up the infrastructure if it is damaged, provide credit, and help restore law and order, but need do little more. In short, the less that real economic development is involved—in the sense of creating the needed elements—and the more that mere reconstruction takes place, the more successful nation building will be.

In contrast, in a country like Afghanistan, where next to none of the elements needed for a modern economy are in place, reference to "reconstruction" is obfuscating. And promising economic development is both self-deluding and misleading to others. There is a very large literature on economic development, and it would be foolhardy to speak about these complex and much-studied processes in a few lines. Hence, just a few observations only on the topic at hand: the ability of external powers to engineer large-scale social change.

Countries that developed over a hundred years or so did draw a great deal on others. For instance, the U.S. industrialization during the 19th century greatly benefited from the importation of a labor force, capital, ideas, and technologies from Europe. But these inputs were sucked in, due to internal dynamics, and not shipped to the United States as part of any plan or of the foreign policy of a nation seeking to develop the United States or to help it do so. The same holds for the four Asian tigers—South Korea, Singapore, Taiwan, and Hong Kong—considered the most successful cases of economic development. The same must be said about China and India. In contrast, the beneficiaries of development assistance from the U.S. Agency for International Development, the World Bank, and from other countries, have been much less able to develop, especially

African and Arabic countries, even when they had great wealth of their own due to oil exports.[25]

The Elements of Economic Reconstruction

What does economic reconstruction require? To answer that, I will draw on a previously published study[26] in which I examined the seven "needs" that were satisfied when the American economy was first developed (roughly 1830 to 1930); showed the ill effects that followed when six of the seven factors involved in satisfying these needs were allowed to deteriorate (from 1950 to 1980); and examined what needed to be done—and a great deal was done—to reconstruct the American economy. Like the elements of democracy, the factors of economic development support each other and rushing one while neglecting the others has a deleterious effect.

- Expeditious transportation of resources and goods
- Effective communication of knowledge and signals
- Secure supplies of power
- Prepared and available human capital (the mobilization and preparation of labor)
- A high level of innovative capacity
- Supportive legal and financial institutions
- The accumulation of capital and capital goods

I suggest that a study of successful reconstruction efforts—such as that of Germany and Japan after World War II—would show that many of the needed elements were in place. Although their economies had deteriorated, they could be relatively readily resupplied and reactivated. In contrast, when one uses the same list to examine the conditions of a country like Afghanistan, it becomes readily evident that economic reconstruction is not possible because most of the needed elements were never in place or only in a very rudimentary amount. Moreover, importing them en masse is not practical. Even in those exceptional conditions in which large-scale economic reconstruction was successful, it took much longer and cost much more than is now commonly implied. Thus, the notion that if the United States simply provided a new Marshall Plan to aid weak economies and countries, they would develop (and democratize on the side), repeated like a mantra,[27] has little validity.

Cultural and Psychological Predispositions: A Shared and Demanding Factor

There is a set of sociological factors that can ease—or severely hinder— all three forms of nation building: unification (pacification included), democratization, and economic reconstruction. The reason this set is often not listed (although it is included in several, more informal, treatments) is because those who invoke it are sometimes considered prejudiced, at the least politically incorrect, or because those who adhere to rationalist schools of social science, according to which self-interest and rational calculating dominate, are blind to this set of factors. The notion that cultural and psychological factors are at work constitutes prejudice only if one assumes that there are some inherent genetic factors that make it impossible for some race or people to become democratic or developed, as some have written about the Arabs (known as Arab exceptionalism).[28] One commonly given reason is that Arabs have a sense of being victims, tend to blame others for their condition, and demand that those others act, rather than place those demands on themselves.

I am merely drawing on the insights of a sociological giant in suggesting that some cultures—which in turn are embedded in personalities— make economic and political development much more difficult than others and are especially resistant to change. To avoid any misunderstanding, I do *not* agree with those who hold that Arabs are congenitally *unable* to develop a liberal democracy; merely that their culture (actually one might better say cultures) will have a much longer and more difficult time doing so than several other cultures. I agree with those who remind us that at one point or another it was said that Japan could not be made democratic or that Catholicism could not be made compatible with a liberal democratic regime. But it takes time and effort. After all, the British and the Americans did not develop democracies overnight under the tutelage of a foreign power. And the conditions in Arab countries are even less favorable for such development than in other Muslim countries.[29]

Max Weber showed that some cultures are less disposed to capitalism—and other features of modernization—than others. Specifically, Catholics, Muslims, and Confucians are less so disposed than Protestants.[30] Culture in this context does not mean art, music, or artifacts, but social and moral values. It is expressed in personality predispositions, especially to save much and work hard, essential for building up a modern economy. What Weber showed for economic development holds for the other elements of nation building. Various scholars have referred to the cultural and psychological factors in different ways.

As I see it—as someone who grew up in the Middle East—the most important value and trait in this respect is self-restraint. It is what allows a person to work hard rather than laze around; save rather than spend; follow rules rather than follow his own whims; refrain from acting violently against those who are different or with whom he disagrees. Self-restraint is not inborn. It is introduced into people who grow up in some cultures (e.g., Britain and Japan), and not in many others. It, by itself, does not guarantee that the nations involved will be unified, democratic, or developed. But it is an important facilitating factor, often downplayed by those who believe, or want to believe, in quickie nation building. Some critics may say that it is Americans who are hedonistic, lascivious, and prone to self-indulgence. However, the foundations for the polity and wealth America now enjoys were laid during the days when Americans worked hard and spent little, and were far from sexually permissive. Even today, Americans have fewer vacation days and holidays than most Europeans and are less permissive.

To the extent that the importance of culture is recognized, it is all too often assumed that one can change cultures quite readily, via communications (Voice of America, the State Department's new "HI magazine," etc.), in what might be called a Madison Avenue approach: change attitudes, values, and habits by sending messages, undertaking educational efforts, developing leadership training, and encouraging cultural exchanges. An example of this approach, which would be humorous if the consequences were not so saddening, is the work of Charlotte Beers, a former public diplomacy chief at the State Department. Under Beers, the State Department developed commercials, websites, and speakers programs to "reconnect the world's billion Muslims with the United States the way McDonald's highlights its billion customers served."[31] According to Robert Satloff of the Washington Institute for Near East Policy, "[t]he results were disastrous."[32] Yet, some people would argue that Beers did not go far enough, "that blitzing Arab and Muslim countries with Britney Spears videos and Arabic-language sitcoms will earn Washington millions of new Muslim sympathizers."[33]

The Madison Avenue approach works only when very large amounts of money are spent to shift people from one product to another when there are next to no differences between them (e.g., two brands of toothpaste) and there is an inclination to use the product in the first place. However, when these methods are applied to changing attitudes about matters as different as condom use[34] and the United Nations,[35] they are less successful. Changing a culture is many hundreds of times more difficult.

Germany and Japan: Exceptions that Prove the Rule

The successful reconstruction and democratization of Germany and Japan after World War II rested on many conditions that are unlikely to be reproduced elsewhere. First of all, they had to be defeated in a war, and then occupied. The occupation lasted longer than many assume. For Japan, occupation lasted nearly seven years; and for Germany, while the occupation lasted four years, full control over foreign relations and trade, industrial production, and military security was not turned over to the Germans until 1955, ten years after the occupation.

Also, many facilitating factors were in much better condition than they are in most other countries in which nation building is attempted. There was no danger that these countries would break up due to a civil war among ethnic groups, as is the case in Afghanistan and Iraq, for instance. No effort had to be expended on unity building. On the contrary, strong national unity was a major reason change could be introduced with relative ease. Other favorable factors included a high level of education, a high income per capita, a sizeable middle class, competent government personnel, and a low level of corruption.[36] Others cite "technical and financial expertise, relatively highly institutionalized political parties, skillful and visionary politicians, well-educated populations, [and] strong national identifications."[37] And there was a strong culture of self-restraint.

Political elements were also more favorable in these two countries. After World War II, Germany and Japan were completely defeated powers whose leaders no longer held sway. The United States had a security interest in these countries, in particular because it was trying to hold off the advance of Communism.

Not only were the conditions in the targeted countries different, but conditions in the United States were different at that time as well. As John W. Dower has argued about the difference between the American occupation of Japan and that of Iraq in 2003, "We do not have the moral legitimacy we had then, nor do we have the other thing that was present when we occupied Japan—the vision of the American public that we would engage in serious and genuinely democratic nation building and that we would do this in the context of an international order."[38]

Both occupations also cost more than is commonly assumed. Further, the commitment level of the United States to reconstruction after World War II was significantly greater than the foreign aid commitment the United States makes today. In 1948, the first year of the Marshall Plan, the aid to the 16 European countries under the Marshall Plan totaled 13 percent of the entire U.S. budget, without even counting money spent in Japan and all of the costs of occupying Germany.[39] In comparison, the Unites States today spends less than one percent of its budget on foreign aid. (Although the United States has pledged billions of dollars to Iraq, most of the funds are dedicated to bolstering security and not to reconstruction.[40])

When all is said and done, suggestions that a Marshall Plan would work for a typical African or Arab country are simply ahistorical.

A Restrained Approach

One may argue that the viewpoint here presented is exceedingly pessimistic—indeed outright discouraging. On the contrary, I believe that there are several good reasons to support many forms of foreign aid to countries in need of it, most of which are humanitarian. Thus, helping nations fight malaria, tuberculosis, and HIV is a good thing, even if it will not significantly contribute to nation building in any sense of the term, and not even stem the pandemic. Vaccinating and feeding children and providing them with elementary schooling is good in itself but should not be dressed up as something else. And surely pacification—preventing genocides of the kind that occurred in Rwanda, halting ethnic cleansing like that in Kosovo, and stopping civil wars, as in Liberia— are fully worthy causes, even if they do not result in nation building.

As far as nation building by external powers is concerned, a much more restrained approach is called for: *an approach that in an optimistic moment greatly narrows the scope of factors it tackles.* As Robert Kaplan suggested, still at least a bit optimistically, "We shouldn't try to fix a whole society; rather, we should identify a few key elements in it, and fix them."[41] It follows that the first criterion by which a restrained policy is to be measured is the scope of its ambition. Does it seek to advance on all three fronts, or limit itself largely to one? And on that front, does it recognize that progress is slow, takes the form of a crab-like walk of at least one step backward for every two forward, and requires a large commitment of resources for long periods of time? Does it recognize that there will be no glory down the road—the new nation (if successfully formed) will not appreciate the help given nor necessarily be an ally of the external power that heavily invested in its construction? The more narrow the goal, the greater the commitment, the lower the expectations, the *more* likely—I do not say it is "likely"—that the approach will make some progress.

Second, *a restrained approach entails initially working with whomever is in power* (as the old regime implodes or is decapitated), rather than starting with dethroning them. This is in sharp contrast to the hyperambitious approach, which assumes that one can undo the warlords, the tribal chiefs, the ethnic leaders, and the religious authorities and replace them with national leaders, often selected and appointed by the external power, and "neutral" professionals and civil servants (one of the first goals of the U.S. occupation of Iraq after May in 2003). In the process, one hopes to shift from tribalism and favoritism to a rule of law that deals with all citizens in the same manner, to move from corruption to transparency, to switch from dealing with contraband, drugs, and guns to serving local and global markets in consumer goods and services. This is, for instance, what the United States tried to do in Afghanistan when it promoted and supported Hamid Karzai as the national head of government and largely refused to deal with the warlords after the war was over, which they largely had helped to win. This is what Britain is trying to do in Bosnia, which is in effect in trusteeship under British rule. This is what the United States and its allies are trying to do in Kosovo. Progress in all these places is hampered by going against the sociological grain, rather than using the lay of the land to change the country gradually.

To put it less metaphorically, over-ambitious societal engineering seeks to overcome prevailing social forces and long-established societal structures and traditions and construct new ones. It tries in vein to quickly undo and then remake deeply ingrained cultural and psychological predispositions, strong emotional ties, and often religious beliefs, as well as powerful reward allocations by tribal chiefs or warlords. A restrained approach would start by dealing with whoever is in power. This is what worked in Germany, where many of the Nazi officials were initially allowed to stay in place because there were few others to run the country—in contrast to the initial attempts to remove all Baath officials, high and low, down to the cop on the beat, in Iraq.

The next step entails hammering out deals and agreements to gain the support of the various warlords or chieftains or mullahs for select

new national efforts, such as building a connecting road or forming the
first units of an integrated national army. Gradually, and often slowly, as
commercial classes increase, middle and professional classes expand;
and as national institutions are able to dispense resources and rewards,
the social forces that support nation building will be enhanced, and the
power of the warlords and their ilk can be scaled back.[42] In addition, the
more the external power allows local people to work things out among
themselves, even if the emerging patterns are not exactly the way things
are done in their home country or do not fit a master plan, the more
likely the new regimes are to develop. Foreign powers would do best if
they limited themselves to setting some broad "do's and don'ts," but
otherwise let "nature" take its course. Details differ from place to place,
but the experience in Iraq, from 2003–2004, illustrates the thesis here
advanced. In Iraq, the United States, under the Coalition Provisional
Authority headed by L. Paul Bremer III, has tried to "do it all." Not
merely were American troops and their few allies training the police,
forming a new army, patrolling cities to prevent looting and other
crimes, ensuring that the various ethnic groups did not fight each other,
and sorting things out among Kurds and Turkmen and Arabs in the
North, but U.S. soldiers were also selecting new "professional" judges
and civil servants, ensuring that no Baaths were among them, taking
sides in fights among various mullahs, firing a media minister for
censoring a local press, trying to jump-start the economy by providing
jobs, renovating schools, drawing up final exams for medical students,
supervising the construction of a women's shelter, and making deliveries
to nursing homes—among many other things.[43]

It might be said that the purpose of all these activities was not to
remake and run the Iraqi society but to gain goodwill. The United
States has long accepted the notion that if you seek to win a war against
local guerillas, you have to win over the support of the civilian population.
There is some merit in the policy (referred to in Latin America as
"Acción Cívica"). However, it too can be readily oversold. Iraqis, for
instance, are a very patriotic people. They have a long and bitter memory

of foreign occupations and caused tens of thousands of casualties to the British when they took over governing Iraq after the collapse of the Ottoman Empire. Providing a few goods and services here and there, even learning to speak a bit of Arabic and gaining some understanding of the local culture—as the Special Forces are trying to do—will not lead Iraquis to accept a government run by a foreign power. Moreover, the scope of the social engineering attempts in Iraq and elsewhere clearly show that much more nation building is being attempted than gaining goodwill. Hence, although there is nothing in the restrained policy to oppose generating goodwill, the notion that it will win over the population at large is unrealistic and, above all, it should not be used to justify an over-ambitions agenda of societal change.

A restrained approach sets priorities: it focuses first and primarily on pacification (to avoid inter ethnic armed conflict) and security (of the American and allied forces) and prevention of support to groups such as Al Qaeda, and of course the production and acquisition of weapons of mass destruction, but initially little more. Developing domestic police forces that are professional rather than political or corrupt—say, by Jordanian standards or even of those of New York City 50 years ago, rather than, say, London's standards today—comes next. All the rest follows gradually, in line with the needs and policies worked out by and with the changing local leaders. If in Iraq this would have meant that a religious regime would have been established in southern Iraq, it would have been left to the Iraqi people who opposed the regime to struggle with it, the way the majority now does with such a regime in Iran. If it would have meant that Baath members would have initially run the civil services, as long as these did not undermine the security of the American forces and allies, it would have been left to the Iraqi people to oppose them or replace them. Gradually, as commerce was restored, thousands of Iraqis who lived in the West repatriated, as the fear of the decommissioned Saddam secret police waned, the demand for various development measures would increase. But these would be driven largely by Iraqis and they would be the address for all things that would not work. The result might well look, for the first years at least, like some kind of mixture between Lebanon and Egypt, maybe like Jordan, at best like Putin's Russia but it would be distinctly better—for all concerned— than the U.S. fate in Vietnam, Somalia, Haiti, Afghanistan, and Iraq. Less is more.

More generally, advocates of nation building would greatly benefit from following the Serenity prayer: "God, grant me the serenity to accept the things I cannot change; the courage to change the things I can; and the wisdom to know the difference." Greatly curtailing foreign ambitions and promises will lead to much greater credibility of these drives and those who make them; will provide stronger domestic support for such efforts among the taxpayers and donors who have to foot the bills; and will pay off by focusing more resources on the few facets that are relatively easy to change rather than tackling numerous facets with little discernible effect.

Notes

Introduction

1. ABC News, *This Week*, 18 November 2001. Senator Patrick Leahy said, "We don't protect ourselves by bending or even shredding our Constitution. We protect ourselves by upholding our Constitution and demonstrating to the rest of the world we will defend ourselves, but we will do it by also defending our own core values."
2. "A Travesty of Justice," *New York Times*, 16 November 2001, A24.
3. See, e.g., Simson Garfinkel, *Database Nation: Death of Privacy in the 21st Century* (Cambridge, MA: O'Reilly, 2000); and Charles J. Sykes, *The End of Privacy* (New York: St. Martin's Press, 1999).
4. See Jay Stanley and Barry Steinhardt, *Bigger Monsters, Weaker Chains: The Growth of an American Surveillance Society* (New York: ACLU, January 2003); Jeffrey Rosen, *The Naked Crowd: Reclaiming Security and Freedom in an Anxious Age* (New York: Random House, 2004).
5. Quoted in Al Knight, "Giving repentance a bad name," *Denver Post* 3 October 2001, B7.
6. Testimony of Attorney General John Ashcroft before the Senate Judiciary Committee on Terrorism, 107th Cong., 1st Sess., 6 December 2001.
7. Ruth R. Wisse, "At Home in Jerusalem," *Commentary*, 115, no.4 (April 2003): 45.
8. See Chapters Nine through Thirteen in Amitai Etzioni, *My Brother's Keeper* (New York: Rowman & Littlefield Publishers, Inc., 2003).
9. Amitai Etzioni, *The Active Society* (New York: The Free Press, 1971).
10. See Chapter Four in *My Brother's Keeper*.
11. For examples of what the Church Commission uncovered, see "Ambiguity between the Clinton White House and CIA with respect to Policy on Osama bin Laden," National Public Radio's *Weekend Edition*, 27 March 2004.
12. For example, the FBI office in Boston protected top Mafia informants even while they continued to commit crimes such as racketeering and murder. See Dick Lehr and Gerard O'Neill, *Black Mass: The Irish Mob, The FBI and A Devil's Deal* (Oxford, U.K.: Public Affairs, 2002).

Chapter 1

1. American Civil Liberties Union, "Insatiable Appetite: The Government"'s Demand for New and Unnecessary Powers after September 11," (Washington, D.C.: American Civil Liberties Union, Washington National Office, April 2002). 1. Available at: http://www.aclu.org/congress/InsatiableAppetite.pdf. Accessed 10/6/02.

2. Wendy Kaminer, "Ashcroft"'s Lies," *American Prospect*, 15 July 2002, 9.

3. *DebatesDebates*, 22 October 2001.

4. Katie Corrigan, *Statement Before the Aviation Subcommittee of the House of Representatives Committee on Transportation and Infrastructure on Passenger Profiling*, 107th Congress, 2nd Session, 27 February 2002.

5. Amitai Etzioni, *The Spirit of Community* (New York, NY: Touchstone, 1993). See also Frederick Schauer, "Slippery Slopes," *Harvard Law Review*, 99 (1985): 361–383.

6. For more, see chapters 2 and 3.

7. See, e.g., Theodore Abel, *The Nazi Movement* (New York, NY: Aherton Press, 1966); Sheri Berman, "Civil Society and the Collapse of the Weimar Republic," *World Politics*, 49, no. 3 (1997): 401–429; Arnold Brecht, *Prelude to Silence* (New York, NY: Howard Fertig, 1968); Peter C. Caldwell and William E. Scheuerman, *From Liberal Democracy to Fascism: Legal and Political Thought in the Weimar Republic* (Boston, MA: Humanities Press, 2000); David Dyzenhaus, "Legal Theory in the Collapse of Weimar: Contemporary Lessons?" *American Political Science Review*, 91 (March 1997): 121–134; E. J. Feuchtwanger, *From Weimar to Hitler: Germany 1918–33* (New York, NY: St. Martin's Press,1993); Ernest Fraenkel, "Historical Obstacles to Parliamentary Government in Germany," in *The Path to Dictatorship: 1918–1913*, trans. John Conway (New York: Praeger, 1967); Peter Fritzsche, "Did Weimar Fail?" *Journal of Modern History*, 68 (September 1996): 629–656; Peter Fritzsche, *Germans Into Nazis* (Cambridge, MA: Harvard University Press, 1998); John Hiden, *Republican and Fascist Germany: Themes and Variations in the History of Weimar and the Third Reich 1918–1945* (New York, NY: Longman, 1996); Hans Mommsen, *The Rise and Fall of Weimar Democracy*, trans. Elborg Forster and Larry Eugene Jones (Chapel Hill, NC: University of North Carolina Press, 1996); A .J. Nicholls, *Weimar and the Rise of Hitler* (New York: St. Martin's Press, 1979); Detlev J. K. Peukert, *The Weimar Republic: The Crisis of Classical Modernity*, trans. Richard Deveson (New York, NY: Hill and Wang, 1992); Kurt Sontheimer, "Anti-Democratic Thought in the Weimar Republic," in *The Path to Dictatorship: 1918–1933*, trans. John Conway (New York: Praeger, 1967), 32–49; and Fritz Stern, "Introduction," in *The Path to Dictatorship: 1918–1933*, trans. John Conway (New York: Praeger, 1967), vii–xxii; Arthur van Riel and Arthur Schram, "Weimar Economic Decline, Nazi Economic Recovery, and the Stabilization of Political Dictatorship," *Journal of Economic History*, 53 (March 1993): 71–105; *Economic Crisis and Political Collapse: The Weimar Republic 1924–1933*. ed. Jurgen Baron von Kruedner (New York, NY: St. Martin's Press, 1990).

8. Fritzsche, *Germans into Nazis*, 1998, 7.

9. Ibid., 8.

10. Abel, *The Nazi Movement*, 1966, 127.

11. Ibid.; Brecht, *Prelude to Silence*, 1968; Fraenkel in *The Path to Dictatorship*,1967; Fritzsche, *Germans into Nazis*, 1998; Nicholls, *Weimar and the Rise of Hitler*, 1979; Kurt Sontheimer in *The Path to Dictatorship*, 1967, 32–49; and Fritz Stern in *The Path to Dictatorship*, 1967, vii–xxii.

12. Abel, *The Nazi Movement*, 1966, 121.
13. Ibid., 166.
14. Ibid., 168–169.
15. Kurt Sontheimer in *The Path to Dictatorship*, 1967, 44.
16. Sheri Berman, *World Politics* 49, no. 3 (1997): 424.
17. Arthur van Riel and Arthur Schram, *Journal of Economic History* 53 (March 1993): 75.
18. Fritz Stern in *The Path to Dictatorship*, 1967, xx.
19. Feuchtwanger, *From Weimar to Hitler: Germany 1918–33*, 1993, 316.
20. Abel, *The Nazi Movement*, 1966; Sheri Berman, *World Politics* 49, no. 3 (1997): 401–429; Brecht, *Prelude to Silence*, 1968; Feuchtwanger, *From Weimar to Hitler: Germany 1918–33*, 1993; Ernest Fraenkel in *The Path to Dictatorship*, 1967; Fritzsche, *Germans into Nazis*, 1998; Hiden, *Republican and Fascist Germany*, 1996; Mommsen, *The Rise and Fall of Weimar Democracy*, 1996; Nicholls, *Weimar and the Rise of Hitler*, 1979; Detlev J. K. Peukert, *The Weimar Republic*, 1992; Arthur van Riel and Arthur Schram, *Journal of Economic History*, 53 (March 1993): 71–105; Kurt Sontheimer in *The Path to Dictatorship*, 1967, 32–49; and Fritz Stern in *The Path to Dictatorship*, 1967, vii–xxii.
21. See Bureau of Transportation Statistics, "Sum: Number of Passengers by Month for 2001."
22. Ibid.
23. Ibid.
24. National Public Radio/Kaiser/Kennedy School Poll on Civil Liberties, 31 October–12 November, 2001.
25. *ABC News/Washington Post* Poll, 11 September 2001. April 1995 and May 1995 figures were also reported in this poll.
26. Pew Center for the People and the Press Poll, 14–17 September 2001. Figures for April 1995 are from a *Los Angeles Times* poll, as reported by the Pew Center.
27. Harris Poll, 13–19 March 2002.
28. For additional discussion, see Amitai Etzioni, "Implications of Select New Technologies for Individual Rights and Public Safety," *Harvard Journal of Law and Technology* 15, no. 2 (Spring 2002): 257–290.
29. *New York Times*/CBS Poll, 15–17 January 1994. Figures reported in Richard L. Berke, "Crime Is Becoming Nation's Top Fear," *New York Times*, 23 January 1994, A1.
30. *New York Times*/CBS Poll, 31 May–3 June 1996. Figures reported in Richard L. Berke, "Poll Indicated Stable Ratings for the President," *New York Times*, 5 June 1996, A1.
31. Richard L. Berke, "Crime Is Becoming Nation's Top Fear," *New York Times*, 23 January 1994, A1.
32. *USA Today*/CNN/Gallup Poll, 13–18 October 1993.
33. *Newsweek* Poll, 7–8 April 1994.
34. Ibid. See Michael Elliott and Peter Annin, "The Crime Debate: Should America Be More Like Singapore?" *Newsweek*, 18 April 2002, 18–22.
35. Rich Connell and Richard A. Serrano, "L.A. Is Warned of New Unrest," *Los Angeles Times*, 22 October 1992, A1.
36. "Beating Case: Tempers Flare at Rally," *USA Today*, 16 April 1996, 3A.
37. Lucy Soto, "Delegation Makes Its Presence Known," *Atlanta Journal and Constitution*, 2 March 1995, 3A.
38. ABC News.com Poll, 31 May–4 June 2000.

39. Ibid.
40. Gallup/CNN/*USA Today* Poll, 23–25 October 1998.
41. Ibid.
42. Federal Bureau of Investigation, U.S. Department of Justice, *Crime in the United States 1998: Uniform Crime Reports,* (Washington, D.C.: GPO, 1999), 10.
43. Federal Bureau of Investigation, U.S. Department of Justice, *Crime in the United States 2000: Uniform Crime Reports,* (Washington, D.C.: GPO, 2001), 11.
44. Federal Bureau of Investigation, U.S. Department of Justice, *Crime in the United States 1995: Uniform Crime Reports,* (Washington, D.C.: GPO, 1996), 10.

Chapter 2

1. Public Law 95-511.
2. 50 U.S.C. 1801(e).
3. 50 U.S.C. 1801(a)(2). See also, Public Law 95-511, 102.
4. Public Law, 107-56, 206. Codified at 50 U.S.C. 1805(c)(2)(B).
5. For a more detailed discussion of these measures, see chapter 3.
6. In 2002, 35,930,611 persons visited the United States. In 2001 it was 39,167,303 persons, and it was 44,608,658 in 2000. Statistics are available from the Commerce Department's Office of Travels and Tourism Department's website at: http://www.tinet.ita.doc.gov/research/monthly/arrivals/index.html?ti_cart_cookie= 20030514.131857.09754. Accessed 14/5/03.
7. Prepared remarks of Attorney General John Ashcroft before the Senate Judiciary Committee Hearing, "The Terrorist Threat: Working Together to Protect America," 108th Congress, 1st Session, 4 March 2003. Available at: http://www.usdoj.gov/ag/testimony/2003/030403senatejudiciaryhearing.htm. Accessed 9/5/03. Eric Lichtblau, "Secret Warrant Requests Increased in 2003." New York Times, May 2, 2004, A17.
8. See Department of Justice, *Field Guide on the New Authorities (Redacted) Enacted in the 2001 Antiterrorism Legislation,* section 216. Available at: http://www.epic.org/privacy/terrorism/DOJ_guidance.pdf. Accessed 29/1/02.
9. Public Law 107-56, 214. Codified at 50 U.S.C. 1842.
10. U.S. Department of Justice, "Remarks of Attorney General John Ashcroft," 30 May 2002. Available at: http://www.justice.gov/ag/speeches/2002/53002agpreparedremarks. htm. Accessed 25/3/03.
11. U.S. Department of Justice, "Remarks of Attorney General John Ashcroft," 30 May 2002. Available at: http://www.justice.gov/ag/speeches/2002/53002agpreparedremarks. htm. Accessed 25/3/03.
12. U.S. Department of Justice, "Remarks of Attorney General John Ashcroft," 30 May 2002. Available at: http://www.justice.gov/ag/speeches/2002/53002agpreparedremarks. htm. Accessed 25/3/03. Attorney General Ashcroft said that prior to the new guidelines the FBI was unable to "simply walk into a public event or a public place to observe ongoing activities." Prepared testimony of Attorney General Ashcroft before the Senate Committee on the Judiciary Concerning Oversight of the Department of Justice, 107th Congress, 2nd Session, 25 July 2002. Available at: http://www.justice.gov/ag/testimony/2002/072502agtestimony.htm. Accessed 12/5/03. In this testimony, Attorney General Ashcroft said, "Agents were barred from researching public information or visiting public places unless they were investigating a specific crime."

13. Toni Locy, Kevin Johnson, and Richard Willing, "Al-Qaeda Records Solve Many 9/11 Puzzles, But Others Linger," *USA Today*, 29 August 2002, 1A. The article quotes a senior U.S. investigator as saying that the hijackers "knew the mosques were out of bounds, and they used them accordingly."

14. See, e.g., Sandra Contenta, "The Hamburg Connection," *Toronto Star*, 29 September 2002, B1; Peter Finn, Hamburg's Caldron of Terror," *Washington Post*, 11 September 2002, A1; Kevin Johnson and Richard Willing, "Array of Unknowns Still Troubling U.S.," *USA Today*, 8 March 2002, 4A; Dirk Laabs and Terry McDermott, "Prelude to 9/11," *Los Angles Times*, 27 January 2003, Sect. 1, p. 1; and Susan Schmidt and Dan Eggen, "Suspected Planner of 9/11 Attacks Captured in Pakistan after Gunfight," *Washington Post*, 14 September 2002, A1.

15. Toni Locy, Kevin Johnson, and Richard Willing, "Al-Qaeda Records Solve Many 9/11 Puzzles, But Others Linger," *USA Today*, 29 August 2002, A. See also, Mini Basu, "Atlanta Muslims Recoil after Federal Raids," *Atlanta Journal-Constitution*, 13 July 2002, 1A.

16. "US, Inquiry Said to Focus on 2 Mosques in Seattle," *New York Times*, 13 July 2002. 1A A8; and Karen Branch-Brioso and Peter Shinkle, "U.S. Looks for Local Terror Ties, Sources Say," *St. Louis Post-Dispatch*, 20 January 2003, A1.

17. Julian Borger, "FBI uses new powers to bug anti-war groups," *Guardian* (London), 24 November 2003, 16.

18. Eric Lichtblau, "U.S. Uses Terror Law to Pursue Crimes From Drugs to Swindling," *New York Times*, 28 September 2003, A1.

19. David Haldane, "Laguna Hills Woman, 20, is Ordered to Federal Prison for Threats She Made during a Hawaiian Cruise. Defense Attorney Calls the Sentence Unfair" *Los Angeles Times*, 23 September 2003, B1.

20. Prepared testimony of Attorney General Ashcroft before the Senate Committee on the Judiciary Concerning Oversight of the Department of Justice, 107th Congress, 2nd Session, 25 July 2002. Available at: http://www.justice.gov/ag/testimony/2002/072502 agtestimony.htm. Accessed 12/5/03.

21. Prepared testimony of Attorney General Ashcroft before the Senate Committee on the Judiciary Concerning Oversight of the Department of Justice, 107th Congress, 2nd Session, 25 July 2002. Available at: http://www.justice.gov/ag/testimony/2002/072502 agtestimony.htm. Accessed 12/5/03.

22. Eric Lichtblau, "U.S. Acts to Use New Power to Spy on Possible Terrorists," *New York Times*, 24 November 2002, A1. See also, Attorney General Ashcroft news conference transcript regarding decision of foreign intelligence surveillance court of review. Available at: http://www.usdoj.gov/ag/speeches/2002/111802fisanewsconference.htm. Accessed 9/5/03.

23. Prepared testimony of Attorney General Ashcroft before the Senate Committee on the Judiciary Concerning Oversight of the Department of Justice, 107th Congress, 2nd Session, 25 July 2002. Available at: http://www.justice.gov/ag/testimony/2002/072502 agtestimony.htm. Accessed 12/5/03.

24. Public Law 104-208, 641. Codified at 8 U.S.C. 1372.

25. Dan Eggen and Cheryl W. Thompson, "INS to Monitor Foreign Students," *Washington Post*, 11 May 2002, A10.

26. Public Law 107-56, 416. The Department of Justice was appropriated $36,800,000 to get SEVIS up and running by January 1, 2003.

27. The U.S. Citizenship and Immigration Services (USCIS) took over the functions and responsibilities of the INS on March 1, 2003, when the Department of Homeland Security was established.

28. Michael Arnone, "Database to Track Foreign Students Still Is Not Ready, Government Reports Finds," *Chronicle of Higher Education*, 24 March 2003; Michael Arnone, "Reorganization of U.S. Agencies Leaves Colleges Worried about How Foreign Students Will Be Treated," *Chronicle of Higher Education*, 7 March 2003; Karen Branch-Brioso, "Foreign-Student Database Is Testing Colleges in Area," *St. Louis Post Dispatch*, 7 April 2003, A1; Sarah Hebel, "Proposed Rules on Foreign Students Leave Many Colleges Worried," *Chronicle of Higher Education*, 26 October 2001, A29–A30; George Lardner, Jr., "Views Differ on System for Tracking Foreign Students," *Washington Post*, 3 April 2003, A8; Diana Jean Schemo, "Problems Slow Tracking of Students from Abroad," *New York Times*, 23 March 2003, B12; and Kelly St. John, "Colleges Grapple with Government Tracking System for Foreign Students," *San Francisco Chronicle*, 14 April 2003, B8.

29. Department of Justice Press Release, "National Security Entry-Exit Registration System." 5 June 2002. Available at: http://www.usdoj.gov/ag/speeches/2002/natlsecentryexittrackingsys.htm. Accessed 14/5/03.

30. Robert S. Mueller, III, "Prepared Remarks Delivered to the Citizens Crime Commission of New York City," The Milstein Lecture, New York, NY, 19 December 2002, Available at: http://www.fbi.gov/pressrel/speeches/milsteinlecture.htm. Accessed 12/5/03. Mueller said: "September 11 made the prevention of terrorist attacks the FBI's top priority and overriding focus. While we remain committed to our other important national security and law enforcement responsibilities, the prevention of terrorism takes precedence in our thinking and planning; in our hiring and staffing; in our training and technologies; and, most importantly, in our investigations. . . . The FBI has always been a collector of intelligence in pursuing its criminal cases. But with the mandate of prevention, we are now restructuring to provide proper analysis and dissemination of intelligence to all our partners in the war on terror."

31. White House, Fact Sheet: "Strengthening Intelligence to Better Protect America." Available at: http://www.whitehouse.gov/news/releases/2003/01/20030128-12.html. Accessed 12/5/03. It states: "Immediately after September 11, the President directed the FBI and the Attorney General to make preventing future terrorist attacks against the homeland their top priority—and they have responded."

32. Department of Justice Press Release, "5000 Interviews Status Report." Available at: http://www.usdoj.gov/opa/pr/2001/December/01_ag_663.htm. Accessed 12/5/2003.

33. News Conference, Attorney General Transcript, "DOJ to seek Death Penalty Against Moussaoui," Miami, FL, 28 March 2002. Available at: http://www.usdoj.gov/ag/speeches/2002/032802newsconferenceaginmiamifloridamoussaoui.htm. Accessed 14/7/04.

34. Prepared Remarks of Attorney General John Ashcroft, "Success and Strategies in the Effort to Liberate Iraq," 17 April 2003. Available at: http://www.justice.gov/ag/speeches/2003/041703effortsliberateIraq.htm. Accessed 12/5/03.

35. See, e.g. Robert Hanssen.

36. Department of Defense, "Fact Sheet: Department of Defense Order on Military Commissions," 21 March 2002. Available at: http://www.defenselink.mil/news/Mar2002/d20020321fact.pdf. Accessed 13 May 2003. See also, Katharine Q. Seeyle,

"Government Sets Rules for Military on War Tribunals," *New York Times,* 21 March 2002, A1; and "Pentagon's Tribunal Plan," *Washington Post,* 22 March 2002, A9.

37. At the time of this writing in April 2004, the Pentagon has announced that it intends to try two detainees held at Guantanamo Bay, Cuba in military tribunals later this year. Neither of the detainees are American citizens. For further information, see K. L. Vantran, "Guantanamo Detainees Charged with Conspiracy to Commit War Crimes, American Forces Information Service News Articles, 24 February 2004. Available at: http://www.defenselink.mil/news/Feb2004/n02242004_200402246.html. Accessed 31/3/04.

38. *USA Freedom Corps,* 30 January 2002, p. 17. Available at: http://www.usafreedomcorps.gov/usafreedomcorps.pdf. Accessed 15/3/02.

39. *USA Freedom Corps,* 30 January 2002. Available at: http://www.usafreedomcorps.gov/usafreedomcorps.pdf . Accessed 15/3/02.

40. Public Law 107-296, 880.

41. Randy Kennedy, "You Looking at Me? Yes, but It's Part of a Plan to Fight Terrorism," *New York Times,* 25 March 2003, D3.

42. Ibid.

43. New York Governor's Office, Press Release, "24/7 Hotline Gathers Information from the Public About Suspected Terrorist Activity," 16 September 2002. Available at: http://www.state.ny.us/governor/press/year02/sept16_1_02.htm. Accessed 13/5/03.

44. Public Law 103-322, 120005. Codified at 18 U.S.C. 2339A. Later changed slightly in Pub. Law 104-132, 1225. Also codified at 18 U.S.C. 2339A.

45. Public Law 104-132, 303, and 323. Codified at 18 U.S.C. 2339B and 2339A.

46. Section 805 of the USA PATRIOT Act (Public Law 107-56) expanded the existing material support law by adding "expert advice or assistance" to the list of actions that are forbidden.

47. 18 U.S.C. 2339A(b).

48. The Holy Land Foundation's assets were frozen by the Treasury Department in 2001. See Judy Keen and Matthew Kalman, "U.S. Raids Texas Charity Called Front for Hamas," *USA Today,* 5 December 2001, 8A. People associated with the organization were arrested. See Toni Locy, "U.S. Hunts 'Terrorist Money Men,'" *USA Today,* 19 December 2002, 3A; and Eric Lichtblau and Judith Miller, "5 Brothers Charged With Aiding Hamas," *New York Times,* 19 December 2002, A19.

49. *Humanitarian Law Project v. United States Department of Justice,* Ninth Circuit Court of Appeals, decided 3 December 2003. Docket Nos. 02-55082, 02-55083.

50. *Humanitarian Law Project, et al. v. John Ashcroft, et al.,* United States District Court, Central District of California, decided 26 January 2004. Case No: CV 03-6107 ABC (MCx).

51. *Padilla v. Rumsfeld,* Second Circuit Court of Appeals, decided 18 December 2003. Docket Nos. 03-2235, 03-2438.

52. Eric Lichtblau, "U.S. Says It Has Not Used New Library Records," *New York Times,* 19 September 2003, A20. Though in Spring, 2004 Ashcroft was compelled to declassify a justice department memo that asked a secret intelligence court to access people's library and business records. Whether or not that request was approved by the court is classified. See Amy Goldstein, "PATRIOT Act Provision Invoked, Memo Says" *Washington Post,* Friday 18 June 2004, A11.

53. Public Law 107-296, 705.

54. Public Law 107-296, 222. Another method of accountability is Section 1001(3) of the PATRIOT Act, which permits the Office of the Inspector General to conduct a bi-annual review of civil liberties violations allegedly committed by the Justice Department. After investigating 1,073 complaints for their July 17, 2004 report, the OIG found 34 new credible civil rights violations. See U.S. Department of Justice Office of the Inspector General, "Report to Congress on Implementation of Section 1001 of the USA PATRIOT Act" Washington, DC, 17 July 2003.

55. HR. 4633 and S. 3107 (107th Congress).

56. Markle Task Force on National Security in the Information Age, *Creating a Trusted Network for Homeland Security* (New York, NY: Markle Foundation, December 2003), Appendix A.

Chapter 3

1. U.S. Constitution, Amendment. IV.

2. Senator Hatch, during the discussion of the USA PATRIOT Act on the Senate floor warned: "I think of the civil liberties of those approximately 6,000 people who lost their lives, and potentially many others if we don't give law enforcement the tools they need to do the job." *Congressional Record* S11023–11024 (daily ed. Oct. 23, 2001) (statement of Sen. Hatch).

3. Nadine Strossen, Remarks at the Communitarian Dialogue on Privacy v. Public Safety (26 November 2001) (transcript available from the Communitarian Network) [hereinafter, Strossen remarks].

4. I refer to a zone because I don't claim that there is a precise point of balance one can identify at which the government tilts clearly in one direction or the other.

5. See The New Golden Rule, *supra note 6*, chapters 1 and 2. For more discussion of the responsive communitarian position, see the "Responsive Communitarian Platform," available at http://www.communitariannetwork.org/platformtext.htm (last modified October 1991); Amitai Etzioni, *The New Golden Rule* (New York: Basic Books, 1996); and Amitai Etzioni, *The Limits of Privacy* (New York: Basic Books, 1999). For a critical treatment, see Elizabeth Frazer, *The Problems of Communitarian Politics* (Oxford, U.K.: Oxford University Press, 1999).

6. For additional discussion of such criteria, see Amitai Etzioni, *The Spirit of Community* (New York: Touchstone, 1993), 177–190; *The New Golden Rule supra note 6*, at 51–55; and *The Limits of Privacy* supra note 6, at 10-55.

7. Richard A. Posner, "Security versus Civil Liberties," *The Atlantic Monthly*, December 2001, at 46.

8. James Murry, *Wireless Nation* (Cambridge, MA: Perseus, 2001), 20 and 313.

9. According to Philip C. W. Sih, although early fax technology was developed in the 19th century, and the U.S. military began using well-developed fax machines during World War II, it was not until the 1970s that the integration of new modem, computer and telephone technologies created the circumstances for a "fax explosion." Philip C. W. Sih, *Fax Power* (New York: Van Nostrand Reinhold, 1993), 1–5.

10. Peter Salus, *Casting the Net* (Reading, MA: Addison-Wesley, 1995), 82–83.

11. The decision in the Supreme Court case of *United States v. New York Tel. Co.* notes that "a pen register is a mechanical device that records the numbers dialed on a telephone by monitoring the electrical impulses caused when the dial on the telephone is

released." *United States v. New York Tel. Co.*, 434 U.S. 159, 161 n.1 (1977). The decision in *United States v. Giordano* notes that a pen register is "usually installed at a central telephone facility [and] records on a paper tape all numbers dialed from [the] line" to which it is attached. *United States v. Giordano*, 416 U.S. 505, 549 n. 1 (1974).

12. Murry, *supra note 12*, at 20, 313.
13. Nielsen/Net Rating for July 2001. Available at: www.nielsen-netrating.co. Accessed 6/12/01.
14. 18 U.S.C. 3122, 3123.
15. 18 U.S.C. 2518.
16. *Smith v. Maryland*, 442 U.S. 735 (1979) [hereinafter Smith] established that the use of a pen register to obtain the numbers dialed from a telephone did not constitute a search under the Fourth Amendment, and therefore did not require a warrant. The court held that "it is doubtful that telephone users in general have any expectation of privacy regarding the numbers they dial, since they typically know that they must convey phone numbers to the telephone company and that the company has facilities for recording this information and does in fact record it for various legitimate business purposes."
17. Peter Swire writes: "The term 'pen register' comes from the old style for tracking all of the calls originating from a single telephone. At one point, the surveillance technology for wiretapped phones was based on the fact that rotary clicks would trigger movements of a pen on a piece of paper." Peter Swire, *Administration Wiretap Proposal Hits the Right Issues But Goes,* Brookings Institution Analysis Paper #3, *America's Response to Terrorism* (The Brookings Institution, Washington, D.C.) 3 October 2001 [hereinafter Swire].
18. Omnibus Crime Control and Safe Streets Act of 1969, Public Law No. 90-351, 82 Stat. 197, 211 (1968) (codified as amended at 18 U.S.C. §§ 2510-2521 (1982 and Supp. IV 1986) [hereinafter Title III].
19. 18 U.S.C. 2518 (1)(b)(ii)(1982 and Supp. IV 1986).
20. Rep. Nancy Pelosi, on CNN Novak, Hunt and Shields., 27 October 2001.
21. Victoria Toensing Remarks at the Communitarian Dialogue on Privacy v. Public Safety (26 November 2001) (transcript available from the Communitarian Network) [hereinafter Toensing remarks].
22. For a discussion of the various analogies applied, see Lt. Col. Joginder Dhillon and Lt. Col. Robert Smith, "Defensive Information Operations and Domestic Law: Limitations on Government Investigative Techniques" *Air Force Law Review,* 56 (2001): 149[hereinafter Dhillon].
23. Ibid.
24. The U.S. Code defines a pen register as a "device which records or decodes electronic or other impulses which identify the numbers dialed or otherwise transmitted on the telephone line to which such device is attached." 18 USC 3127(3) (1994).
25. Swire, *supra note 21.*
26. Ibid.
27. Field Guide on the New Authorities (Redacted) Enacted in the 2001 Anti-Terrorism Legislation. Available at: http://www.epic.org/privacy/terrorism/DOJ_guidance.pdf section. Accessed: 29/1/02 [hereinafter DOJ Field Guide], 216A.
28. Electronic Communications Privacy Act, Pub. L. 99-508, 100 Stat. 1848 (1986) [hereinafter, ECPA].

29. The ECPA extended the section of the U.S. Code requiring a court order to intercept oral or wire communications to include electronic communications.18 U.S.C. 2511, as amended by ECPA title I, secs. 101(b), (c)(1), (5), (6), (d), (f)[(1)], 102.

30. For further discussion, see Terrence Berg, "www.wildwest.gov: The Impact of the Internet on State Power to Enforce the Law," *Brigham Young University Law Review* (2000): 1305; James X. Dempsey, "Communications Privacy in the Digital Age: Revitalizing the Federal Wiretap Laws to Enhance Privacy," *Albany Law Journal of Science & Technology*, 8 (1997): 65; Dhillon, *supra note 25* ; Susan Freiwald, "Uncertain Privacy: Communications Attributes Under the Digital Telephony Act," *Southern California Law Review*, 69: 949 (March 1996); and Paul Taylor, "Issues Raised by the Application of the Pen Register Statutes to Authorize Government Collection of Information on Packet-Switched Networks," *Virginia Journal of Law & Technology*, 6 (2001): 4.

31. Christian David Hammel Schultz, "Unrestricted Federal Agent: Carnivore and the Need to Revise the Pen Register Statute," *Notre Dame Law Review* 76 (June 2001): 1221–1223.

32. Swire *supra note 21.*

33. See 18 U.S.C.A. 2703 (West 2000), which reads: (a) Contents of electronic communications in electronic storage. A governmental entity may require the disclosure by a provider of electronic communication service of the contents of an electronic communication, that is in electronic storage in an electronic communications system for more than 180 days or less, only pursuant to a warrant issued under the Federal Rules of Criminal Procedure or equivalent State warrant.

34. 18 U.S.C. 2703(a).

35. DOJ Field Guide, *supra note 30,* section 220.

36. An oft-repeated anecdote that illustrates the point: At the launch of Jini, a wireless device that has the potential to track a user's movements, Sun Microsystems CEO Scott McNealy responded to privacy concerns with the declaration that "You have zero privacy now. Get over it!" For a further discussion, see Jeffrey Rosen, *The Unwanted Gaze: The Destruction of Privacy in America* (New York: Knopf, 2001.)

37. See Etzioni, *The Limits of Privacy, supra note 6,* Chapter 3.

38. Deborah Russell and G. T. Gangemi Sr., *"Encryption"* in *Building in Big Brother,* ed. Lance Hoffman (Santa Clara, CA: Springer, Verlag Publishers, 1995), 11.

39. Dorothy E. Denning and William E. Baugh Jr., *Encryption and Evolving Technologies as Tools of Organized Crime and Terrorism* (U.S. Working Group on Organized Crime, National Strategy Information Center, 1997).

40. Jonathan Krim, "High-tech RBI Tactics Raise Privacy Questions," *The Washington Post,* 14 August 2001, at A01 [hereinafter Krim].

41. Steven Levy, *Crypto: How the Code Rebels Beat the Government—Saving Privacy in the Digital Age* (New York: Viking, 2001) [hereinafter Levy], 310—311.

42. In practice, it is difficult to make the information completely secure, just as it is difficult to completely delete files. For example, if the operating system needs to perform another task while an encryption application is in progress, it will halt the application temporarily and return to it later. Before it halts the program, it writes the encryption application and its key to disk as a safety measure. When the application is completed later, many users do not realize that a version of the unencrypted key will remain on the disk until the computer writes it over. Bruce Schneier, *Applied Cryptography,* (New York, NY: Wiley, 1994), 148.

43. FBI Director Louis J. Freeh stated that: "From 1995-1996, there was a two-fold increase (from 5 to 12) in the number of instances where the FBI's court-authorized electronic efforts were frustrated by the use of encryption that did not allow for law enforcement access." *Hearing on Encryption Before the Senate Committee on the Judiciary*, 107th Congress (2001) (statement of Louis J. Freeh, Director, Federal Bureau of Investigation) [hereinafter Freeh statement]. See also, *The Limits of Privacy*, 1999, *supra note 6*, Chapter Three.

44. I wrote "seems" because it is not possible to know whether the National Security Agency has found a way to decrypt high-power encryption. However, the great efforts made to gain keys reinforce the view that the NSA has failed in its endeavors to this effect.

45. See John Perry Barlow, *Cyberspace Independence Declaration*, issued 9 February 1996. Available at: http://www.eff.org/~barlow/Declaration-Final.html. Accessed 22/1/02; and Steven Levy, "The Battle of the Clipper Chip," *New York Times*, 12 June 1994.

46. FBI Director Louis J. Freeh testified that: "The looming specter of the widespread use of robust, virtually untraceable encryption is one of the most difficult problems confronting law enforcement as the next century approaches. At stake are some of our most valuable and reliable investigative techniques, and the public safety of our citizens. We believe that unless a balanced approach to encryption is adopted that includes a viable key management infrastructure, the ability of law enforcement to investigate and sometimes prevent the most serious crimes and terrorism will be severely impaired." Freeh statement, *supra note 48*.

47. Roving wiretaps were initially introduced in the ECPA, *supra note 31*.

48. 18 U.S.C. 2518 (11)(b) (1994 Supp. IV). The addition of this section was part of the ECPA.

49. 18 U.S.C. 2518 (11)(b)(i) (1994 Supp. IV).

50. 18 U.S.C. 2518 (11)(b) (1994).

51. Intelligence Authorization Act for Fiscal 1999, Public Law No. 105-272, 604, 112 Stat. 2396, 2413 (1998), amending 18 U.S.C. 2518 (11)(b)(1994).

52. The most significant case is that of *United States v. Petti*, 973 F.2d 1441, 1444–1445 (9th Cir. 1992) [hereinafter Petti]. For further discussion, see also Bryan R. Faller, "The 1998 Amendment to the Roving Wiretap Statute: Congress 'Could Have' Done Better," *Ohio State Law Journal* 60 (1999): 2093.

53. The USA PATRIOT Act, *supra note 1*, section 206 (amending 50 U.S.C. 1805(c)(2)(B)).

54. Hearing on the Foreign Intelligence Surveillance Act of 1978 Before the Subcommittee on Criminal Laws and Procedures of the Senate Committee on the Judiciary, 95th Congress, 1st Session, 13 (1977), reprinted in 1978 ISKCON 3904, 3916.

55. Tom Ricks, "A secret US court where one side always seems to win," *Christian Science Monitor*, 21 May 1982.

56. The USA PATRIOT Act, *supra note 1*, section 218 (amending 50 U.S.C. 1804(a)(7)(B), 1823(a)(7)(B)). See also 147 Congressional Record S11004.

57. Department of Justice overview of the USA PATRIOT Act, as entered into the *Congressional Record* S11055 (daily ed. Oct. 25, 2001) [hereinafter DOJ Overview].

58. 50 U.S.C. 1806.

59. William Carlsen, "Secretive US court may add to power," *San Francisco Chronicle*, 6 October 2001.

60. The USA PATRIOT Act, *supra note 1*, sections 214, 216 (amending 50 U.S.C. 1842, 1843 and 18 U.S.C. 3121, 3123, 3127).
61. Ibid., section 216 A. See also DOJ Field Guide, *supra note 30*, section 216A.
62. The law is worded in a peculiar way, saying that a single order can be used at any carrier's facility, but not explicitly establishing that the order has nationwide scope. Ibid., section 216A.
63. Ibid., section 220 (amending 18 U.S.C. 2703).
64. Ibid., section 220. See also DOJ Field Guide, *supra note 30*, section 220.
65. See Etzioni, *The Limits of Privacy, supra note 6*, Chapter 3; Levy, *supra note 45*, at 226–268.
66. See, e.g., Bruce W. McConnell and Edward J. Appal, Draft paper, "Enabling Privacy, Commerce, Security and Public Safety in the Global Information Infrastructure." Available at: http://www.epic.org/crypto/key_escrow/white_paper.html. Accessed: 29/1/02; and *Hearing on Privacy in a Digital Age: Encryption and Mandatory Access Before the Senate Committee on the Judiciary, Subcommittee on the Constitution, Federalism, and Property Rights*, 105th Congress (1998) (statement of Robert S. Litt, Principal Associate Deputy Attorney General). For a fuller history of key escrow, see A. Michael Froomkin, "It Came from Planet Clipper: The Battle over Cryptographic Key 'Escrow,'" *University of Chicago Law Forum*, 15 (1996).
67. Jedi Callusing, "White House Yields a Bit on Encryption," *New York Times*, 8 July 1998, D1; Lance J. Hoffman, *Encryption Policy for the Global Information Infrastructure*, statement at the Eleventh International Conference on Information Security, Cape Town South Africa, 9–12 May 1995.
68. The USA PATRIOT Act, *supra note 1*, section 412.
69. AG Order No. 2529-2001, 66 *Fed. Reg.* (31 October 2001) (to be codified at 28 CAR pt. 500-501).
70. Military Order of 13 November 2001, Detention, Treatment, and Trial of Certain Non-Citizens in the War against Terrorism. 66 *Fed. Reg.* 57831–57836 (16 November 2001).
71. Senator Patrick Leahy, ABC News, *This Week*, (Burwell's Information Services, 18 November 2001): "We don't protect ourselves by bending or even shredding our Constitution. We protect ourselves by upholding our Constitution and demonstrating to the rest of the world we will defend ourselves, but we will do it by also defending our own core values."
72. Morton Halperin, "Less Secure Less Free," *The American Prospect*, 19 November 2001, 10.
73. Hearing on the Department of Justice and Terrorism Before the Senate Committee on the Judiciary, 107th Congress (2001) (statement of Sen. Hatch).
74. *Olmstead v. United States*, 277 US 438 (1928).
75. Ibid., 466.
76. *Katz v. United States*, 389 US 347 (1967) [hereinafter, Katz] at 351.
77. Ibid., 351.
78. Ibid., 361.
79. See, e.g., Anthony G. Amsterdam, "Perspectives on the Fourth Amendment," *Minnesota Law Review* 58, no. 349 (1974): 384–385; Richard S. Julie, "High-tech Surveillance Tools and the Fourth Amendment: Reasonable Expectation of Privacy in the Technological Age," *Criminal Law Review* 37, no. 127 (2000): 131–133; Jonathan Todd Laba, "If You Can't Stand the Heat, Get Out of the Drug Business: Thermal

Imagers, Emerging Technologies, and the Fourth Amendment," *California Law Review* 84 (1996): 1470–1475; Scott E. Sundby, "'Everyman's' Fourth Amendment: Privacy or Mutual Trust between Government and Citizen?," *Columbia Law Review* (1994): 1751; *State v. Reeves*, 427 So. 2nd at 425 (Dennis, J., dissenting).

80. *United States v. Maxwell*, 45 M.J. 406 (C.A.A.F. 1996).

81. *United States v. Charbonneau*, 979 F. Supp. 1177 (S.D. Ohio 1997).

82. Dhillon, *supra note 26* at 150.

83. Smith *supra note 20*. For further discussion of the implications of *Smith* for seizure of electronic communications, see the Department of Justice search and seizure manual, *Searching and Seizing Computers and Obtaining Electronic Evidence in Criminal Investigations*, Computer Crime and Intellectual Property Section, Criminal Division, U.S. Department of Justice (January 2001). Available at: http://www.usdoj.gov: 80/criminal/cybercrime/searchmanual.wpd. Accessed: 24/1/02.

84. Dhillon *supra note 26*, at 150.

85. U.S. Constitution, Amendment IV.

86. Petti *supra note 56*, citing *Maryland v. Garrison*, 480 U.S. 79, 84, 94 L. Ed. 2d 72, 107 S. Ct. 1013 (1987).

87. Ibid., citing *United States v. Turner*, 770 F.2d 1508, 1510 (9th Cir. 1985).

88. The U.S. Code specifies that in the case of a roving intercept, "the order authorizing or approving the interception is limited to interception only for such time as it is reasonable to presume that the person identified in the application is or was reasonably proximate to the instrument through which such communication will be or was transmitted." 18 U.S.C. 1518 (11)(b)(iv); and that the interception "shall not begin until the place where the communication is to be intercepted is ascertained by the person implementing the interception order." 18 U.S.C 1518 (12).

89. *Steagald v. United States*, 451 U.S. 204 (1981).

90. Tracey Maclin, "Another grave threat to liberty," *National Law Journal*, 12 November 2001, A20.

91. Clifford S. Fishman, "Interception of Communication in Exigent Circumstances: The Fourth Amendment, Federal Legislation, and the United States Department of Justice," *Georgia Law Review* 22 no. 1 (Fall 1987) [hereinafter Fishman]: 65–69.

92. Solicitor General Ted Olsen, on CNN, *Larry King Live*, 24 October 2001.

93. Nadine Strossen, on CNN *News, International.*, 30 October 2001.

94. Bart Kosko, "Your Privacy is a Disappearing Act," *Los Angeles Times*, 2 December 2001, M5.

95. Adam Clymer, "Anti-terrorism bill passes, U.S. gets expanded powers," *New York Times*, 26 October 2001, A1.

96. Strossen remarks, *supra note 4*.

97. Alan Dershowitz, on CNN *News, International*, 30 October 2001.

98. *The USA-PATRIOT ACT Boosts Government Powers While Cutting Back on Traditional Checks and Balances.* (ACLU, Leg. Analysis). Available at: http://www.aclu.org/congress/l110101a.html. Accessed17/1/02.

99. Letter from Assistant Director John Collingwood to Members of Congress, 16 August 2000. Available at: http://www.fbi.gov/congress/congress00/collingwood081600.htm. Accessed 29/1/02.

100. Illinois Institute of Technology Research Institute, *Independent Review of Carnivore System—Final Report* (2000). Available at: http://www.epic.org/privacy/carnivore/

carniv_final.pdf. Accessed: 29/1/02. [hereinafter IITRI Report], at 3.4.4.1.1, 3.4.4.1.4, 3.4.4.1.6.

101. Ibid., 3.4.4.1.3.

102. *Fourth Amendment Issues Raised by FBI's "Carnivore" Program: Hearing Before the House Subcomm. on the Constitution of the House Comm. on the Judiciary*, 106th Congress 1 (2001) (statement of Donald M. Kerr, Assistant Dir. Lab. Div. FBI) [hereinafter July 2000 Kerr statement].

103. *The "Carnivore" Controversy: Electronic Surveillance and Privacy in the Digital Age: Hearing before the Senate Comm. on the Judiciary*, 106th Congress 3 (2000) (statement of Donald M. Kerr, Assistant Dir. Lab. Div. FBI) [hereinafter Sept. 2000 Kerr statement].

104. July 2000 Kerr statement, *supra note 107*.

105. Aff. of Randall S. Murch, U.S. District Court District of New Jersey, *United States v. Scarfo* (4 October 2001). Available at: http://www.epic.org/crypto/scarfo/murch_aff.pdf. Accessed 29/1/01 [hereinafter Murch Aff.].

106. In his affidavit during the Scarfo trial, FBI's Randall Murch explains that the public encryption key is usually a long string of computer data that the user cannot simply memorize. Instead, the user has a passphrase that enables him to decrypt his files. When the passphrase is entered into a dialog box, the program then decrypts the key and then uses it to decrypt the file. Ibid.

107. "Judge Orders Government to Explain How 'Key Logger' System Works," *Computer and Online Industry Litigation Reporter*, 14 August 2001, 3.

108. Order to search Merchant Services of Essex County, filed 8 May 1999. U.S. Court District, District of New Jersey. Available at: http://www2.epic.org/crypto/scarfo/order_5_99.pdf. Accessed 1/29/01 [hereinafter Scarfo warrant].

109. The component that records the keystrokes can be set to evaluate each keystroke individually before recording it. When a keystroke is entered, KLS checks the status of the computer's communication ports. The component will only record a keystroke if all the communications ports are inactive. Murch Aff., *supra note 110*.

110. Michael Froomkin, "The Metaphor is the Key: Cryptography, the Clipper Chip, and the Constitution," *University of Pennsylvania Law Review* 143 (Jan. 1995): 709.

111. Hiawatha Bray, "Military-Tech Complex," *Boston Globe*, 29 November 2001, C1.

112. Ted Bridis, "FBI develops new tools to ensure government can eavesdrop on high-tech messages," *Associated Press*, 21 October 2001.

113. Bob Port, "Spy Software Helps FBI Crack Encrypted Mail," *Daily News*, 9 December 2001, 8.

114. Lou Doliner, "With new tools, authorities can target suspects' computers with accuracy," *Newsday*, 12 December 2001, C08.

115. Hearing on Protecting Constitutional Freedoms from Infringement by Counterterrorism Efforts Before the Subcomm. on the Constitution, Federalism, and Property Rights of the Sen. Comm. on the Judiciary Committee, 107th Congress (2001) (statement of Jerry Berman, Exec. Dir. Center for Democracy and Technology) [hereinafter Berman statement].

116. See ACLU, "Urge Congress to Stop the FBI's Use of Privacy-Invading Software" (2000). Available at: http://www.aclu.org/action/carnivore107.html. Accessed 1/10/02 [hereinafter ACLU].

117. See Aaron Kendal, "Carnivore: Does the Sweeping Sniff Violate the Fourth Amendment?," *T.M. Cooley Law Review* 18 (Trinity Term 2001):183.

118. See ACLU, *supra note 121*.

119. "FBI eavesdrops on e-mail, crashed privacy barriers," *USA Today*, 24 July 2000, 16A.

120. Tom Bridis, "Congressional Panel Debates Carnivore as FBI Moves to Mollify Privacy Worries," *Wall Street Journal*, 25 July 2000, A28.

121. IITRI Report, *supra note 105*, at ES.5 - E.S.6.

122. Ibid., ES.5.

123. Ibid., xi and xiv.

124. Ibid., ix, xiii.

125. John Schwartz, "Wiretapping System Works on Internet, Review Finds," *New York Times*, 22 November 2000, A19.

126. IITRI Report, *supra note 105*, at 3.4.4.1.

127. For an example of the neo-Luddite position, see Chellis Glendinning, "Notes Toward a Neo-Luddite Manifesto," *Utne Reader*, Mar./Apr. 1990. For an historical discussion of Luddism, see Kirkpatrick Sale, *Rebels Against the Future* (Reading, MA: Addison-Wesley, 1995).

128. Brief of the United States in Opposition to Defendant's Pre-trail Motions, *United States v. Scarfo*, (July 2001) Available at: http://www2.epic.org/crypto/scarfo/gov_brief.pdf/. Accessed 29/1/02 [hereinafter Scarfo brief].

129. Motion to Suppress Evidence Seized by the Government Through the Use of a Keystroke Logger, *United States v. Scarfo*, (June 2001). Available at: http://www2. epic.org/crypto/scarfo/def_supp_mot.pdf. Accessed: 29/1/02.

130. Scarfo warrant, *supra note 113*.

131. Richard Willing, "FBI technology raises privacy issues," *USA Today*, 31 July 2001, 3A.

132. Scarfo brief, *supra note 133*, at 38.

133. Opinion and Order in the case of *United States v. Scarfo et al.*, issued 26 December 2001. Available at: http://lawlibrary.rutgers.edu/fed/html/scarfo2.html-1.html. Accessed 29/1/02.

134. Amitai Etzioni, *The Spirit of Community*, Chapter Six, Etzioni, *The New Golden Rule*, *supra note 6*, Chapters One and Two.

135. *The Economist* reports that the anti-terrorism bill released by the United Kingdom's home secretary David Blunkett on November 13 includes a provision that would give public authorities the power to force protestors to remove disguises. *Economist*, 17 November 2001, 54.

136. This point was made recently by Jeffrey Rosen in *The Naked Crowd: Reclaiming Security and Freedom in an Anxious Age* (New York: Random House, 2004).

137. Statement of Louis J. Freeh, Director, Federal Bureau of Investigation, before the House Appropriations Committee, Subcommittee on Commerce, Justice, State, Judiciary and Related Agencies, 105th Congress (1998). Available at: http://www.fbi.gov/congress/congress98/hac35.htm. Accessed 29/1/02.

138. Alan Cullison and Andrew Higgins, "How al Qaeda Agent Scouted Attack Sites in Israel and Egypt," *The Wall Street Journal*, 16 January 2002, 1.

139. Levy, *supra note 45*, Chapter 7.

140. 18 U.S.C 1518 (5).

141. 18 U.S.C. 2518 (5) (Supp. IV 1986).

142. See, e.g., *United States v. Clerkley*, 556 F.2nd 709, 717 (4th Cir. 1977); *United States v. Costello*, 610 F. Supp. 1450, 1477 (N.D. Ill. 1985); *United States v. Clemente*, 482 F. Supp. 102. 108–110 (S.D.N.Y. 1979).

143. *Scott v. United States*, 436 US 128 (1978).

144. Ibid., 137–39.

145. Ibid., 142.

146. Bob Barr, "A Tyrant's Toolbox: Technology and Privacy in America," *Journal of Legislation* 26 (2000): 71.

147. IITRI Report, *supra note 105*, at 3.4.4.1.6, ES.5.

148. Ibid., 3.4.4.1.3.

149. Dan Eggen and Brook Masters, "U.S. Indicts Suspect in September 11 Attack," *Washington Post*, 12 December 2001, A01.

150. Berman statement, *supra note 120*.

151. William Carlson, "Secretive US Court may add to power," *San Francisco Chronicle*, 6 October 2001, A3.

152. Berman statement, *supra note 120*.

153. Private communication with Orin Kerr, Washington, D.C., 14 December 2001.

154. Toensing remarks, *supra note 25*.

155. 50 U.S.C. 1804(a).

156. "Law enforcement, rather than a Court, will decide what is 'content' and systems like Carnivore will be used without any real judicial supervision." ACLU, *More on ACLU Objections to Select Provisions of Proposed Anti-Terrorism Legislation*, (2001). Available at: http://www.aclu.org/congress/Patriot_Links.html. Accessed 17/1/02.

157. *United States v. Rodriguez*. 968 F. 2d 130, 135 (2d Cir. 1992).

158. *Boyd v. United States*, 116 U.S. 616 (1886).

159. *Weeks v. United States*, 232 U.S. 383 (1914).

160. See, e.g., *United States v. Leon*, 468 U.S. 897 (1984), which established a "good faith" exception to the exclusionary rule; *Nix v. Williams*, 467 U.S. 431, 444 (1984), which created the "inevitable discovery" exception to the exclusionary rule; *Massachusetts v. Sheppard*, 468 U.S. 981 (1984), upholding the "good faith" exception; *United States v. Calandra*, 414 U.S. 338, 348 (1974), which establishes that the exclusionary rule does not proscribe use of *all* illegally obtained evidence. For further discussion, see Leslie-Ann Marshall and Shelby Webb Jr., "Constitutional Law—The Burger Court's Warm Embrace of an Impermissibly Designed Interference with the Sixth Amendment Right to the Assistance of Counsel—The Adoption of the Inevitable Discovery Exception to the Exclusionary Rule: *Nix v. Williams*", *Howard Law Journal* 28, no. 1 (1985): 945; Christopher A. Harkins, "The Pinocchio Defense Witness Impeachment Exception to the Exclusionary Rule: Combating a Defendant's Right to Use with Impunity the Perjurious Testimony of Defense Witnesses," *University of Illinois Law Review* 375 (1990): 389–411.

161. "The process that brought you this bill is terribly flawed. After bypassing a Judiciary Committee mark-up, a few Senators and their staffs met behind closed doors, on October 12, 2001 to craft a bill. The full Senate was presented with anti-terrorism legislation in a take-it-or-leave-it fashion with little opportunity for input or review. No conference committee met to reconcile the differences between the House and Senate versions of the bill. We find it deeply disturbing that once again the full Senate will be forced to vote on legislation that it has not had the opportunity to read. Senate offices are closed and staff cannot even access their papers to fully prepare you for this important vote. Regular order is being rejected and it is an offense to the thoughtful legislative procedures necessary to protect the Constitution and Bill of Rights at a time when

the rights of so many Americans are being jeopardized." Letter from Laura Murphy, Dir. ACLU Washington, D.C. Office to Senate, Urging Rejection on Final Version of the USA PATRIOT Act, 23 October 2001. Available at: http://www.aclu.org/congress/1102301k.html. Accessed: 17/1/02.

162. Sen. Orin Hatch said before Congress that: "We can never know whether these tools would have prevented the attack on America, but, as the Attorney General has said, it is certain that without these tools we did not stop the vicious acts of last month. I personally believe that if these tools had been in law—and we have been trying to get them there for years—we would have caught those terrorists. If these tools could help us now to track down the perpetrators—if they will help us in our continued pursuit of terrorists—then we should not hesitate to enact these measures into law. God willing, the legislation we pass today will enhance our abilities to protect and prevent the American people from ever again being violated as we were on September 11." *Congressional Record*, S11015 (2001) (statement of Sen. Hatch).

163. The House Judiciary Committee held a hearing on the Fourth Amendment Issues Raised by the FBI's Carnivore Program on 24 July 2000. Testimonies are available at: http://www.house.gov/judiciary/con07241.htm. Accessed 22/1/02. The Senate Judiciary Committee held a hearing on Carnivore on 6 September 2000. Testimonies are available at: http://www.senate.gov/~judiciary/wl96200f.htm. Accessed: 22/1/02.

164. Press Release, "ACLU, in Unique Tactic, ACLU Seeks FBI Computer CodeOn 'Carnivore' and Other Cybersnoop Program" 14 July 2000. Available at: http://www.aclu.org/news/2000/n071400a.html. Accessed 29/1/02.

165. Press Release, "EPIC, Lawsuit Seeks Immediate Release of FBI Carnivore Documents" 2 Aug. 2000. Available at: http://www.epic.org/privacy/carnivore/8_02_release.html. Accessed 29/1/02.

166. Nick Wingfield and Don Clark, "Internet Companies Decry FBI's E-mail Wiretap Plan," *The Wall Street Journal*, 12 July 2000, B12.

167. Opinion and Order requiring submission of report "detailing how the key logger device function," U.S. District Court, District of New Jersey, *United States v. Scarfo*, (August 2001. Available at: http://www2.epic.org/crypto/scarfo/order_8_7_01.pdf. Accessed 29/1/02.

168. John Schwartz, "U.S. Refuses to Disclose PC Tracking," *New York Times*, 25 August 2001, C1.

169. Krim, *supra note 44*.

170. See 114 *Congressional Record* 14, 750 (1968).

171. *Official Report of the Senate Select Committee on Intelligence*, headed by Senator Frank Church, as published in *US News and World Report*, 15 December 1975, 61.

172. Jim McGee, "The Rise of the FBI," *Washington Post Magazine*, 20 July 1997, W10.

173. 50 U.S.C. 1803.

174. Robert O. Keohane, "Governance in a Partially Globalized World," *American Political Science Review* 95, no. 1 (2001): 1–13.

175. Martin Edmonds, *International Affairs* 62, no. 2 (1986): 290-91 (reviewing *Military Intervention in Democratic Societies*, eds. Peter J. Rowe and Christopher J. Whelan); Jeffrey Simpson, "What Happens when Society's Guardians Need Guardians Themselves?" *Globe and Mail* (Canada), 11 September 1996.

176. Seymour Martin Lipset and William Schneider, *The Confidence Gap: Business, Labor, and Government in the Public Mind* (Baltimore, MD: Johns Hopkins University Press, 1987.)

Chapter 4

1. Bilahari Kausikan, "Asian versus 'Universal' Human Rights," *The Responsive Community* 7, no. 3 (summer 1997): 9–21.

2. John Stuart Mill argues: "But neither one person, nor any number of persons, is warranted in saying to another human creature . . . that he shall not do with his life for his benefit what he chooses to do with it." John Stuart Mill, *On Liberty,* ed. David Spitz (New York: W.W. Norton, 1975), 71.

3. *The Responsive Communitarian Platform: Rights and Responsibilities,* (Washington, D.C.: The Communitarian Network, 1991). For more information, visit: http://www.gwu.edu/~ccps; Ezekiel Emanuel, *The Ends of Human Life: Medical Ethics in a Liberal Polity* (Cambridge, MA: Harvard University Press, 1991), chapter 6; Amitai Etzioni, *The New Golden Rule: Community and Morality in a Democratic Society* (New York: Basic Books, 1996); Mark Kuczewski, "Organ Donation and the Common Good," paper presented at Communitarian Perspectives on Bioethics, Washington, D.C., 5 June 2001; Paul Lauritzen, et al., "The Gift of Life and the Common Good: The Need for a Communal Approach to Organ Procurement," *Hastings Center Report* 31, no. 1 (2001): 29–35.

4. Amitai Etzioni, *The Spirit of Community: The Reinvention of American Society* (New York: Crown Publishers, Inc., 1993), 177–191.

5. Daniel A. Bell, "Together Again?," review of *The Spirit of Community,* by Amitai Etzioni, *Times Literary Supplement* (London, U.K.) 11 November 1994, 5–6.

6. See numerous essays since 1990 in *The Responsive Community: Rights and Responsibilities.* Amitai Etzioni, *The New Golden Rule: Community and Morality in a Democratic Society* (New York: Basic Books, 1996).

7. Amitai Etzioni, *A Comparative Analysis of Complex Organizations,* rev. ed. (Glencoe, IL: Free Press, 1975).

8. Amitai Etzioni, *The Limits of Privacy* (New York: Basic Books, 1999).

9. Robert Pear, "Bush Accepts Rules to Protect Privacy of Medical Records," *New York Times,* 13 April 2001, A1; Robert Pear, "New Privacy Rules Are Challenged," *New York Times,* 21 December 2000, A22; and Anthony Shadid, "US Bolsters the Power of Patients to Guard Privacy of Personal Data," *Boston Globe,* 13 April 2001, A3.

10. Judith Miller, Stephen Engelberg, and William Broad, *Germs: Biological Weapons and America's Secret War* (New York: Simon & Schuster, 2001).

11. Rebecca Katz argues that the threat of bioterrorism is "more real than at any time in the nation's history" and yet as it "stands today, a biological weapons attack would quickly overwhelm the public health system." See Rebecca Katz, "Public Health Preparedness: The Best Defense against Biological Weapons" *Washington Quarterly* 25, no. 3 (Summer 2002): 81.

12. Congress, Senate, Committee on Health, Education, Labor and Pensions, "Testimony of the American Public Health Association Concerning the Need For Investment in Public Health Preparedness to Combat Terrorism," 107th Cong., 1st sess., 9 October 2001.

13. Jonathan Rauch, "Countering the Smallpox Threat," *Atlantic Monthly,* December 2001.

14. Centers for Disease Control and Prevention, National Immunization Program, "Anthrax Vaccine: What You Need to Know," November 2000. Available at: http://www.cdc.gov/nip/publications/VIS/vis-anthrax.pdf. Accessed 21/11/01.

15. Department of Defense. "Anthrax Vaccine Immunization Program." Available at: http://www.anthrax.osd.mil/HTML_interface/default.html. Accessed 30/11/01.

16. The World Health Organization, Communicable Disease and Surveillance Response, "WHO Fact Sheet on Smallpox," October 2000. Available at: http://www.who.int/emc/diseases/smallpox/factsheet.html. Accessed 29/11/01.

17. The World Health Organization, Communicable Disease and Surveillance Response, "WHO Fact Sheet on Smallpox," October 2000. Available at: http://www.who.int/emc/diseases/smallpox/factsheet.html. Accessed 29/11/01.

18. Department of Defense, "Anthrax Vaccine Immunization Program." Available at: http://www.anthrax.osd.mil/HTML_interface/default.html. Accessed 30/11/01.

19. Judith Miller, Stephen Engelberg, and William Broad, *Germs: Biological Weapons and America's Secret War* (New York: Simon & Schuster, 2001), 190, 265.

20. Jennifer Peck, "Prickly Issue—Fluoride or No—Hits Wayland; Determined Group Fights Health Board Move," *Boston Globe*, 13 September 1998, A1.

21. Jane E. Brody, "For the Vaccine-Wary, a Lesson in History," *New York Times*, 3 October 2000, F8; "Measles Risk Linked to Gap in Vaccinations," *New York Times*, 16 August 1996, A16; and John O'Neil, "When Parents Say No to Vaccinations," *New York Times*, 2 January 2001, F6.

22. Mark Granovetter, "Economic Action and Social Structure: A Theory of Embeddedness," *American Journal of Sociology* 91, no. 3 (1985), 481–510; and Michael J. Sandel, *Liberalism and the Limits of Justice* (Cambridge, U.K. Cambridge University Press, 1982).

23. For an additional discussion on shaming, see Amitai Etzioni, "Is Shaming Shameful?" in *The Monochrome Society* (Princeton, NJ: Princeton University Press, 2001), 37–47.

24. Michael T. Osterholm and John Schwartz, *Living Terrors: What America Needs to Know to Survive the Coming Bioterrorist Catastrophe* (New York: Delacorte Press, 2000), 85–87.

25. Donald. A. Henderson, Thomas V. Inglesby, John G. Bartlett, Michael S. Aschet, et al., "Smallpox as a Biological Weapon: Medical and Public Health Management," *The Journal of the American Medical Association*, 9 June 1999, 2127–2137; and D.A. Henderson, "Bioterrorism as a Public Threat," *Emerging Infectious Diseases* 4, no. 3 (July/September 1998). See the discussion of the "Dark Winter" exercise which was carried out in the summer of 2001 at Andrews Air Force Base, in Shannon Brownlee, "Why America Isn't Ready for Bioterrorism," *New Republic*, 29 October 2001, 22–24.

26. Michael T. Osterholm and John Schwartz, *Living Terrors: What America Needs to Know to Survive the Coming Bioterrorist Catastrophe* (New York: Delacorte Press, 2000), 141–143.

27. Donald. A. Henderson, Thomas V. Inglesby, John G. Bartlett, Michael S. Aschet, et al., "Smallpox as a Biological Weapon: Medical and Public Health Management," *Journal of the American Medical Association*, 9 June 1999, 2127–2137.

28. Donald. A. Henderson, Thomas V. Inglesby, John G. Bartlett, Michael S. Aschet, et al., "Smallpox as a Biological Weapon: Medical and Public Health Management," *Journal of the American Medical Association*, 9 June 1999, 2127–2137.

29. Donald. A. Henderson, Thomas V. Inglesby, John G. Bartlett, Michael S. Aschet, et al., "Smallpox as a Biological Weapon: Medical and Public Health Management," *Journal of the American Medical Association*, 9 June 1999, 2127–2137.

30. Michael T. Osterholm, and John Schwartz, *Living Terrors: What America Needs to Know to Survive the Coming Bioterrorist Catastrophe* (New York: Delacorte Press, 2000), 141.

31. Anthony H. Cordesman, *Defending America: Asymmetric Terrorist Attacks with Biological Weapons*, (Washington, D.C.: Center for Strategic and International Studies, 2001), 28. Available at: http://www.csis.org/homeland/reports/biotechterrorasym.pdf. Accessed 21/11/01. Thomas V. Inglesby, Tara O'Toole, and Donald A. Henderson, "Preventing the Use of Biological Weapons: Improving Response Should Prevention Fail," *Clinical Infectious Diseases* 30 (2000): 926–929.

32. Jessica Stern, *The Ultimate Terrorists* (Cambridge, MA: Harvard University Press, 1999).

33. Congress, Senate, Foreign Relations Committee, "Hearing on the Threat of Bioterrorism and the Spread of Infectious Diseases: Testimony of Donald A. Henderson," 5 Septembe 2001. Available at: http://www.hopkins-biodefense.org/pages/library/spread.html. Accessed 7/11/01.

34. Lawrence O. Gostin, *Public Health Law: Power, Duty, Restraint* (Berkeley, CA University of California Press, 2000).

35. Ibid., 212–213.

36. Ibid., 213.

37. Nicholas Confessore, "In Bed with Bob Barr: How Conservatives Became the ACLU's Best Friends," *American Prospect*, 5 November 2001. For more information about the coalition of organizations, see the "In Defense of Freedom" website at http://www.indefenseoffreedom.org.

38. Lawrence O. Gostin, Scott Burris, and Zita Lazzarini, "The Law and the Public's Health: A Study of Infectious Disease Law in the United States," *The Columbia Law Review* 99 (January 1999): 59–128.

39. Alan Wolfe, *Moral Freedom: The Impossible Idea that Defines the Way We Live Now* (New York: W.W. Norton, 2001).

40. Robert Bellah, et al., *Habits of the Heart: Individualism and Commitment in American Life* (Berkeley: University of California Press, 1985).

41. Ronald Bayer, *Private Acts, Social Consequences: AIDS and the Politics of Public Health* (New York: Free Press, 1989).

42. Ibid.

43. "SARS Fact Sheet: Isolation and Quarantine" Centers for Disease Control. Available at: http://www.cdc.gov/ncidod/sars/pdf/isolationquarantine.pdf. Accessed 23/10/03. Additionally, the Centers for Disease Control drafted bold new measures to contain a SARS outbreak, including isolating SARS patients, closing mass transit, business, and schools and enforcing curfews. For more on these proposals, see Betsy McKay, "U.S. Weights Quarantines for SARS," *Wall Street Journal*, 20 October 2003, A3.

44. See Henry L. Davis, "Beating Back Microbes/ Confronting the Specter of Flu, SARS, even Bioterrorism," *Buffalo News*, 29 December 2003; and Paul Gustafson, "A Quiet Study of New Quarantine Law," *Minneapolis Star Tribune*, 2 February 2004.

45. National Public Radio, All Things Considered, "US Preparedness to Deal with Biological Warfare," 23 October 2001.

46. Avram Goldstein, "Bioterror Self-Triage Hopes to Avert Panic" *Washington Post*, 14 July 2003, B1.

47. "The Community's Pulse," *The Responsive Community* 12, no.1 (2001/2002): 95.

48. Congress, Senate, Committee on Health, Education, Labor and Pensions, "Testimony of the American Public Health Association Concerning the Need For Investment in Public Health Preparedness to Combat Terrorism," 107th Cong., 1st Sess., 9 October 2001.

49. Laurie Garrett, "Responding to the Nightmare of Bioterrorism," *The Responsive Community* 12, no.1 (2000/2001): 88–93.

50. Laurie Garrett, *Betrayal of Trust: The Collapse of Global Public Health* (New York: Hyperion, 2000), 538–539; and Michael T. Osterholm and John Schwartz, *Living Terrors: What America Needs to Know to Survive the Coming Bioterrorist Catastrophe* (New York: Delacorte Press, 2000), 162.

51. Laurie Garrett, "Responding to the Nightmare of Bioterrorism," *The Responsive Community* 12, no.1 (2000/2001): 88–93.

52. Ibid.

53. John Duffy, *The Sanitarians: A History of American Public Health* (Urbana, IL: University of Illinois Press, 1990).

54. Laurie Garrett, *Betrayal of Trust: The Collapse of Global Public Health* (New York: Hyperion, 2000), 435.

55. Fitzhugh Mullan, "Silent Killers," review of *The Coming Plague: Newly Emerging Diseases in a World Out of Balance*, by Laurie Garrett, *Los Angeles Times*, 6 November 1994, 3.

56. Personal communication with Fitzhugh Mullan.

Chapter 5

1. See, for example, Mark Helm, "As Term Nears End, Armey Not Afraid to Speak His Mind," *Washington Post*, 18 August 2002, A7; Bill Miller, "Homeland Security Cost Weighed," *Washington Post*, 17 July 2002, A8; and Bill Miller and Juliet Eilperin, "House GOP Leaders Unveil Homeland Bill," *Washington Post*, 19 July 2002, A4.

2. This is not to say that no one is in favor of national ID cards. For compelling arguments in favor of such devices, see A. Michael Froomkin, "The Uneasy Case for National ID Cards as a Means to Enhance Privacy," Draft paper, March 2004; Joseph W. Eaton, *The Privacy Card: A Low Cost Strategy to Combat Terrorism* (Lanham, MD: Rowman and Littlefield, 2003); and Nicholas Kristof, "May I See Your ID?," *New York Times*, 17 March 2004, A25.

3. Robert Ellis Smith, "The True Terror is in the Card," *New York Times Magazine*, 8 September 1996, 59.

4. American Civil Liberties Union, "The ACLU on . . . National Identification Cards," 1996. Available at http://www.aclu.org/library/aaidcard.html. Accessed 3/4/04.

5. The Phyllis Schlafly Report, "Liberty vs. Totalitarianism, Clinton-Style," *The Phyllis Schlafly Report*, July 1998, 1–3.

6. John J. Miller and Stephen Moore, "A National ID System: Big Brother's Solution to Illegal Immigration" (Washington, D.C.: Cato Institute, 7 September 1995).

7. See, for example, Ibid., 5, 6, 20.

8. In 2003, 40.4 million persons visited the United States. In 2002, it was 35,930,611 persons, and it was 39,167,303 in 2001. Statistics are available from the Commerce Department's Office of Travels and Tourism Department's website at: http://www.tinet. ita.doc.gov/research/monthly/arrivals/index.html?ti_cart_cookie=20030514.131857.0 9754. Accessed 14/5/03.

9. Prepared testimony of Robert J. Cramer, Managing Director, Office of Special Investigations, General Accounting Office, before the House Judiciary Subcommittee on Immigration, Border Security, and Claims on Counterfeit Documents Used to Enter the United States From Certain Western Hemisphere Countries Not Detected, 108th Congress, 1st Session, 13 May 2003 (GAO-03-713T).

10. Prepared testimony of Robert J. Cramer, Managing Director, Office of Special Investigations, General Accounting Office, before the Senate Committee on Finance on Weaknesses in Screening Entrants Into the United States, 108th Congress, 1st Session, 30 January 2003 (GAO-03-438T); and Prepared testimony of Robert J. Cramer, Managing Director, Office of Special Investigations, General Accounting Office, before the House Judiciary Subcommittee on Immigration, Border Security, and Claims on Counterfeit Documents Used to Enter the United States From Certain Western Hemisphere Countries Not Detected, 108th Congress, 1st Session, 13 May 2003 (GAO-03-713T).

11. Prepared testimony of Robert H. Hast, Assistant Comptroller General for Investigations, Office of Special Investigations, General Accounting Office, before the House Judiciary Subcommittee on Crime on Breaches at Federal Agencies and Airports, 106th Congress, 2nd Session, 25 May 2000 (GAO/T-OSI-00-10).

12. Ibid.

13. Ibid.

14. Ibid., and Letter from Robert H. Hast, Managing Director, Office of Special Investigations, General Accounting Office, to the Honorable Lamar Smith, Chairman of House Judiciary Subcommittee on Crime regarding Security Improvement Inquiry, 31 August 2001 (GAO-01-1069R).

15. Ibid. One agency, the CIA, did not provide a specific response to the inquiry and the other agency, the U.S. Courthouse and Federal Building in Orlando, Florida, was not part of the follow-up. However, the GAO reports it contacted the U.S. Marshals Service and the General Services Administration, which are responsible for the security of judicial facilities and federal buildings.

16. Department of Justice Press Release, "Attorney General Statement Regarding Airport Security Initiative," 23 April 2002. Available at: http://www.usdoj.gov/opa/pr/2002/April/02_ag_246.htm. Accessed 25/6/03.

17. Prepared Testimony of Paul J. McNulty, U.S. Attorney for the Eastern District of Virginia, before the House Judiciary Subcommittee on Crime, Terrorism and Homeland Security and the Subcommittee on Immigration, Border Security and Claims, 107th Congress, 2nd Session, 25 June 2002.

18. Ibid.

19. Office of the Inspector General, Social Security Administration, *Social Security Number Integrity: An Important Link in Homeland Security*, Management Advisory Report, May 2002 (A-08-02-22077).

20. This observation is based on a report given by Robert J. Cramer, Managing Director, Office of Special Investigations, General Accounting Office, to the Markle Task Force on National Security in the Information Age's Sub-group on Reliable Identification for Homeland Protection and Collateral Gains at The George Washington University on 16 June 2003.

21. Prepared testimony of Richard M. Stana, Director, Justice Issues, General Accounting Office, before the House Judiciary Subcommittee on Crime, Terrorism and Homeland Security and Subcommittee on Immigration, Border Security, and Claims on Identity Fraud, 107th Congress, 2nd Session, 25 June 2002 (GAO-02-830T).

22. Ibid.

23. Diane Brooks, "Raids Net Pile of Fake IDs," *Seattle Times*, 14 September 2002, B1.

24. Warren A. Lewis (Interim Director, Washington District Office, Bureau of Immigration and Customs Enforcement, Department of Homeland Security), Letter to the Editor, *Washington Post*, 17 May 2003, A24.

25. Mary Beth Sheridan, "Raids Don't Stop D.C. Street Trade in Fake U.S. IDs," *Washington Post*, 3 August 2003, A1.

26. Prepared testimony of James G. Huse, Jr., Inspector General, Social Security Administration, before the House Judiciary Subcommittee on Crime, Terrorism and Homeland Security and Subcommittee on Immigration, Border Security, and Claims, 107th Congress, 2nd Session, 25 June 2002.

27. Statement of Senator Richard Durbin before the Senate Governmental Affairs Subcommittee on Restructuring and the District of Columbia Subcommittee and Subcommittee on Oversight of Government Management on Fake or Fraudulently Issued Driver's Licenses, 107th Congress, 2nd Session., 16 April 2002.

28. Ibid.

29. Prepared testimony of Paul J. McNulty, U.S. Attorney for the Eastern District of Virginia, before the House Judiciary Subcommittee on Crime, Terrorism and Homeland Security and the Subcommittee on Immigration, Border Security and Claims, 107th Congress, 2nd Session, 25 June 2002.

30. Breeder documents are basic documents that an individual needs to present to obtain other documents, such as driver's licenses or passports. Breeder documents include birth certificates, Social Security cards, and baptismal records.

31. Prepared testimony of Robert J. Cramer, Managing Director, Office of Special Investigations, General Accounting Office, before the Senate Committee on Finance, "Counterfeit Identification and Identification Fraud Raise Security Concerns Statement" 108th Congress, 1st Session, 9 September 2003 (GAO-03-1147T).

32. Mary Beth Sheridan, "Raids Don't Stop D.C. Street Trade in Fake U.S. IDs," *Washington Post*, 3 August 2003, A1.

33. How-to books, such as John Q. Newman, *The Id Forger: Homemade Birth Certificates and Other Documents Explained* (Port Townsend, WA: Loompanics Unlimited, 1999), are available for purchase from mainstream retailers like Amazon.com.

34. See, e.g., Allan Legel, "Ex-Clerk Accused of DMV Fraud," *Washington Post*, 10 January 2003, B2; Christopher Quinn, "Bribery in Driver's Tests?" *Atlanta Journal Constitution*, 19 January 2002, 1A; and Ronald Smothers, "State Report to Outline Lapses in Security at DMV Offices," *New York Times*, 7 November 2002, A28.

35. Prepared testimony of Robert J. Cramer, Managing Director, Office of Special Investigations, General Accounting Office, before the Senate Committee on Finance on Counterfeit Identification and Identification Fraud Raise Security Concerns, 108th Congress, 1st Session, 9 September 2003 (GAO-03-1147T).

36. Ibid.

37. For example, Max Forge, *How to Make Driver's Licenses and Other Id on Your Home Computer*.

38. Prepared Testimony of David C. Myers, Special Agent, Identification Fraud Coordinator, Florida Division of Alcoholic Beverages and Tobacco, Department of Business and Professional Regulation, Fraudulent Identification Unit, before the Senate Governmental Affairs Permanent Subcommittee on Investigations on Phony IDs and Credentials Via the Internet, 106th Congress, 2nd Session, 19 May 2000.

39. Ibid.

40. U.S. Code, vol. 18, sec. 1028 (2003).

41. Prepared Testimony of James H. Huse, Inspector General, Social Security Administration, before the Senate Governmental Affairs Permanent Subcommittee on

Investigations on Phony IDs and Credentials Via the Internet, 106th Congress, 2nd Session, 19 May 2000.

42. See, e.g., http://www.phonyid.com.

43. Prepared testimony of David C. Myers, Special Agent, Identification Fraud Coordinator, Florida Division of Alcoholic Beverages and Tobacco, Department of Business and Professional Regulation, Fraudulent Identification Unit, before the Senate Governmental Affairs Permanent Subcommittee on Investigations on Phony IDs and Credentials Via the Internet, 106th Congress, 2nd Sesion., 19 May 2000.

44. Prepared testimony of John S. Pistole, Acting Assistant Director, Counterterrorism Division, Federal Bureau of Investigation, before the Senate Finance Committee on Homeland Security and Terrorism Threat From Document Fraud, Identity Theft and Social Security Number Misuse, 108th Congress, 1st Session, 9 September 2003.

45. Ibid.

46. For more information about In-Person Proofing at Post Offices, see U.S. Postal Service, Notice, "In-Person Proofing at Post Offices (IPP) Program," *Federal Register*, 68, no. 116 (17 June 2003): 35922–35923.

47. General Services Administration, *Interim E-Authentication Gateway: Concept of Operations* (Falls Church, VA: Prepared by Mitrerek Systems, February 2003), 1. Available at: http://www.cio.gov/eauthentication/documents/ea_conops_21403.pdf. Accessed 25/09/03.

48. Executive Office of the President, Office of Management and Budget Press Release, "OMB And GSA Work to Increase Internet Security for Citizens," 18 July 2003. Available at: http://www.estrategy.gov/documents/eauthenticationnewsrelease.pdf. Accessed 25/9/03.

49. General Services Administration, Request for Comments, "E-Authentication Policy for Federal Agencies," *Federal Register*, 68, no. 133 (11 July 2003): 41371–41373.

50. Federal Identity and Credentialing Committee, "Authentication and Identity Policy Framework for Federal Agencies," Draft Document. Available at: http://www.cio. gov/ficc/documents/FICCframework-draftv6.1.htm. Accessed 26/9/03.

51. Prepared Testimony of Robert J. Cramer, Managing Director, Office of Special Investigations, General Accounting Office, before the Senate Committee on Finance on Counterfeit Identification and Identification Fraud Raise Security Concerns, 108th Congress, 1st Session, 9 September 2003 (GAO-03-1147T).

52. For more information, visit http://www.whitehouse.gov/omb/egov/gtog/evital.htm.

53. Judi Hasson, "Electronic Death Records 'Vital' at SSA," *Federal Computer Week*, 1 April 2002.

54. Under the Personal Responsibility and Work Opportunity Reconciliation Act of 1996, states are to collect the Social Security number of driver's license applicants on their application. See *U.S. Code*, vol. 42, sec. 666a (1996). The GAO reported in 2002 that six states still were not collecting the Social Security numbers of driver's license applicants. See General Accounting Office, *Child Support Enforcement: Most States Collect Driver's SSNs and Use Them to Enforce Child Support*, Report to the Subcommittee on Human Resources, Committee on Ways and Means, House of Representatives, February 2002 (GAO-02-239).

55. Office of the Inspector General, Social Security Administration, *Congressional Response Report: Terrorist Misuse of Social Security Numbers*, October 2001, 5 (A-08-02-32041).

56. General Accounting Office, *Social Security Numbers: Improved SSN Verification and Exchange of States' Driver Records Would Enhance Identity Verification*, Report to Congressional Requesters, September 2003, 1 (GAO-03-920).

57. Institute for Communitarian Policy Studies, *License to Hide: Security Implications of America's Lax Driver's License Laws* (Institute for Communitarian Policy Studies, 2004).

58. General Accounting Office, *Social Security Numbers: Improved SSN Verification and Exchange of States' Driver Records Would Enhance Identity Verification*, Report to Congressional Requesters, September 2003, 10 (GAO-03-920).

59. Such legislation has been proposed in the 108th Congress. For more information, see for example, Congress, House, *Driver's License Integrity Act of 2003*, 108th Congress, 1st Session, 2003, H.R. 1121; and Idem, A Bill to Bar Federal Agencies from Accepting for Any Identification-Related Purpose a State-Issued Driver's License, or Other Comparable Identification Document, Unless the State Requires a License or Comparable Document Issued to a Nonimmigrant Alien to Expire Upon the Expiration of the Alien's Authorized Period of Stay in the United States, 108th Congress, 1st Session, 2003, H.R. 655.

60. Prepared Testimony of Betty Serian, Vice Chair, American Association of Motor Vehicle Administrators, before the Senate Governmental Affairs Subcommittee on Oversight of Government Management Restructuring and the District of Columbia on Improving the Security of Driver's Licenses, 107th Congress, 2nd Session, 16 April 2002.

61. Prepared Testimony of Robert J. Cramer, Managing Director, Office of Special Investigations, General Accounting Office, before the Senate Committee on Finance on Counterfeit Identification and Identification Fraud Raise Security Concerns, 108th Congress, 1st Session, 9 September 2003 (GAO-03-1147T).

62. For more information about the potential benefits of biometric technology, see Shane Ham and Robert D. Atkinson, *Modernizing the State Identification System: An Action Agenda*, Progressive Policy Institute Policy Report, February 2002. Available at: http://www.ppionline.org/documents/Smart_Ids_Feb_02.pdf. Accessed 15/10/03. U.S. Department of Justice, U.S. Department of State, and National Institute of Standards and Technology, *Use of Technology Standards and Interoperable Databases with Machine-Readable, Tamper Resistant Travel Documents*, Report to Congress, January 2003.

63. I am indebted to Eric Benhamou, Chairman of the Board of Directors at 3Com Corporation, Palm Inc., and Cypress Semiconductors, for this point.

64. Personal Communication with Tom Wolfsohn, Senior Vice President, Government Affairs, American Association of Motor Vehicle Administrators, 26 September 2003.

65. Prepared testimony of Keith A. Rhodes, Chief Technologist, Applied Research and Methods, General Accounting Office, before the House Government Reform Subcommittee on Technology, Information Policy, Intergovernmental Relations, and the Census, 108th Congress, 1st Session, 9 September 2003 (GAO-03-1137T).

66. Federal Bureau of Investigation, "Using Technology to Protect Americans," 3 October 2003. Available at: http://www.fbi.gov/page2/iafis100303.htm. Accessed 16/10/03.

67. Jennifer Lee, "Progress Seen in Border Tests of ID System," *New York Times*, 7 February 2003, A14.

68. Mark Townsend and Paul Harris, "Security Role for Traffic Cameras," *Observer* (London), 9 February 2003, 2; and Barnaby J. Feder, "Face-Recognition Technology Improves," *New York Times,* 14 March 2003, C2.

69. I am indebted to Shane Ham, Senior Policy Analyst, with the Technology and New Economy Project at the Progressive Policy Institute, for these points.

70. For more information about the use of smart cards by the government, see Prepared Testimony of Joel C. Willemssen, Managing Director, Information Technology Issues, General Accounting Office, before the House Government Reform Committee's Subcommittee on Technology, Information Policy, Intergovernmental Relations, and the Census, 108th Congress, 1st Session, 9 September 2002 (GAO-03-1108T).

71. Quoted in Benny Evangelista, "Surveillance Society: Don't Look Now, But You May Find You're Being Watched," *San Francisco Chronicle,* 9 September 2002, E1.

72. I am indebted to Eric Benhamou, Chairman of the Board of Directors at 3Com Corporation, Palm Inc., and Cypress Semiconductors, for this point.

73. Larry Ellison, "Digital IDs Can Help Prevent Terrorism," *Wall Street Journal,* 8 October 2001, A26; and Carrie Kirby, "Ellison Again Urges Federal ID Database," *San Francisco Chronicle,* 15 August 2002, B1.

74. Eli Lehrer, "The Case for a Market Based National Identity System," Decision Memorandum published by the Foundation for the Defense of Democracies, November 2002. Available at: http://www.defenddemocracy.org/usr_doc/Market-Based_National_Identity_System.pdf. Accessed 13/8/03.

75. Prepared testimony of Keith A. Rhodes, Chief Technologist, Applied Research and Methods, General Accounting Office, before the House Government Reform Committee's Subcommittee on Technology, Information Policy, Intergovernmental Relations, and the Census, 108th Congress, 1st Session, 9 September 2003 (GAO-03-1137T). For more information, visit http://www.immigration.gov/graphics/shared/lawenfor/bmgmt/inspect/ inspass.htm.

76. Quoted in Jim Getz, "Highway Safety Group Finds Old Debates Have New Context," *St. Louis Post-Dispatch,* 10 September 2002, B1.

77. Federal Trade Commission, Identity Theft Data Clearinghouse, "National and State Trends in Fraud & Identity Theft January-December 2003." Available at: http://www.consumer.gov/ sentinel/pubs/top10fraud2003.pdf. Accessed 7/14/04.

78. Federal Trade Commission, *Identity Theft Survey Report,* prepared by Synovate, September 2003. Available at: http://www.ftc.gov/os/2003/09/synovatereport.pdf. Accessed 10/9/03.

79. Ibid.

80. Federal Bureau of Investigation, "General Frequently Asked Questions." Available at: http://www.fbi.gov/aboutus/faqs/faqsone.htm. Accessed 12/9/02.

81. For a further discussion of this issue, see Amitai Etzioni, *The Limits of Privacy* (New York: Basic Books, 1999), 105.

Chapter 6

1. Pål Kolstø, "Nation-Building and Social Integration Theory," in *Nation-Building and Ethnic Integration in Post-Soviet Societies: An Investigation of Latvia and Kazakstan,* ed. Pål Kolstø (Boulder, CO: Westview Press, 1999), 49.

2. Wendell Bell and Walter E. Freeman, "Introduction," in *Ethnicity and Nation-Building: Comparative, International, and Historical Perspectives*, eds. Wendell Bell and Walter E. Freeman (Beverly Hills, CA: Sage Publications, 1974), 11.
3. Michael Ignatieff, "Nation-Building Lite," *New York Times Magazine*, 28 July 2002, 30.
4. Ibid.
5. Karin von Hippel, "Democracy by Force: A Renewed Commitment to Nation Building," *Washington Quarterly*, 23, no. 1 (2000): 96.
6. Ibid.
7. Seymour Martin Lipset, "Some Social Requisites of Democracy: Economic Development and Political Legitimacy," *American Political Science Review*, 53, no. 1 (1959): 69–105.
8. For an excellent examination of the meaning of "nation," see Margaret Moore, *The Ethics of Nationalism* (New York, NY: Oxford University Press, 2001), 6–9.
9. For more discussion, see Amitai Etzioni, *Political Unification Revisited: Building Supranational Communities* (Lanham, MD: Lexington Books, 2001).
10. Gary T. Dempsey, "Fool's Errands: America's Recent Encounters with Nation Building," *Mediterranean Quarterly*, 12, no. 1 (2001): 59.
11. Minxin Pei and Sara Kasper, "The 'Morning After' Regime Change: Should US Force Democracy Again?," *Christian Science Monitor*, 15 January 2003, 9.
12. Max Boot, "What Next? The Bush Foreign Policy Agenda Beyond Iraq," *Weekly Standard*, 5 May 2003, 29.
13. Max Boot, "Against All Odds," *Weekly Standard*, 22 March 2004.
14. Jim Yardley, "Democracy, Chinese Style: 2 Steps Forward, 1 Step Back," *New York Times*, 21 December 2003, sec. 1, p. 3.
15. William Safire, "Creeping Democracy," *New York Times*, 22 March 2004, A23.
16. Pamela Constable, "Afghan Harmony Hard to Find," *Washington Post*, 9 February 2004, A14; Carlotta Gall, "For More Afghan Women, Immolation Is Escape," *New York Times*, 8 March 2004, A1.
17. Minxin Pei and Sara Kasper, "Lessons from the Past: The American Record on Nation Building," *Policy Brief No. 24*, May 2003. Available at: http://www.ceip.org/files/pdf/Policybrief24.pdf. Accessed 01/08/03.
18. Thomas Carothers, quoted in George Packer, "Dreaming of Democracy," *New York Times Magazine*, 2 March 2003, 60.
19. Graham Allison, "Deepening Russian Democracy: Progress and Pitfalls in Putin's Government," *Harvard International Review*, 24, no. 2 (2002): 63–64.
20. Archie Brown, "Russia and Democratization," *Problems of Post-Communism*, 46, no. 5 (1999): 5–6.
21. Thomas Carothers, "Creating Democracy in Iraq," interview by Warren Olney, *To The Point*, ed. Kyle McKinnon. Public Radio International. KCRW, Santa Monica, 16 April 2003.
22. Robert A. Dahl, *Polyarchy: Participation and Opposition* (New Haven, CT: Yale University Press, 1971), 3.
23. Adeed Dawisha and Karen Dawisha, "How to Build a Democratic Iraq," *Foreign Affairs*, 82, no. 3 (2003): 47.
24. The *Journal of Democracy* is published by Johns Hopkins University Press.
25. See, for instance, William Easterly, Ross Levine, and David Roodman, "New Data, New Doubts: Revisiting 'Aid, Policies, and Growth,'" *Center for Global Development*

Working Paper No. 26, June 2003. Available at: http://www.cgdev.org/wp/cgd_wp026. pdf. Accessed 8/9/03.

26. Amitai Etzioni, *An Immodest Agenda: Rebuilding America Before the 21st Century* (New York: New Press, 1983).

27. See, inter alia, Stephen E. Ambrose, "The Master (Nation) Builder," *National Review*, 11 March 2002, 30–32; Bob Geldof, "A Continent in Crisis: We Must Act Now to Prevent Apocalypse," *The Observer* (London), 15 June 2003, 20; Gordon Brown, "Marshall Plan for the Next 50 Years," *Washington Post*, 17 December 2001, A23.

28. Alfred Stepan and Graeme B. Robertson, "An 'Arab' More Than 'Muslim' Electoral Gap," *Journal of Democracy*, 14, no. 3 (2003): 29–44.

29. Ibid.

30. Max Weber, *The Protestant Ethic and the Spirit of Capitalism*, trans. Talcott Parsons (New York: Scribner, 1958); idem, *Economy and Society: An Outline of Interpretive Sociology*, trans. Ephraim Fischoff et al., eds. Guenther Roth and Claus Wittich (New York: Bedminster Press, 1968); and idem, *The Religion of China: Confucianism and Taoism*, trans. and ed. Hans H. Herth (New York: Free Press, 1951).

31. Robert Satloff, "How to Win Friends and Influence Arabs," *Weekly Standard*, 18 August 2003, 18.

32. Ibid.

33. Ibid.

34. For instance, the Centers for Disease Control conducted a 10-year ad campaign to educate Americans about condoms and to encourage their use to prevent HIV transmission. After spending millions of dollars on these ads, a CDC study found that only 45 percent of sexually active high school students used a condom the last time they had sex. Jeffry Scott, "Condom Ads Get Direct: Use Them and Get Sex," *The Atlanta Journal and Constitution*, 3 October 1994, B1. A recent evaluation of the program issued an unqualified "no" in answer to the question "Has the U.S. federal government's HIV/AIDS television [public service announcement] campaign been designed not only to make the public aware of HIV/AIDS but also to provide appropriate messages to motivate and reinforce behavior change?," William DeJong, R. Cameron Wolf, and S. Bryn Austin, "U.S. Federally Funded Television Public Service Announcements (PSAs) to Prevent HIV/AIDS: A Content Analysis," *Journal of Health Communication*, 6 (2001): 256. Of the 56 ads reviewed, 50 were created by the CDC; the other 6 were created by the National Institute on Drug Abuse.

35. Shirley A. Star and Helen MacGill Hughes, "Report on an Educational Campaign: The Cincinnati Plan for the United Nations," *Journal of American Sociology*, 55 (1950): 389–400, quoted in Bernard Berelson and Gary A. Steiner, *Human Behavior: An Inventory of Scientific Findings* (New York: Harcourt, Brace & World, 1964), 530.

36. Marina Ottaway, "Nation Building," *Foreign Policy*, 132 (Sept./Oct. 2002): 17.

37. Robert A. Packenham, *Liberal America and the Third World* (Princeton, NJ: Princeton University Press, 1973) 34–35.

38. John W. Dower, quoted in George Packer, "Dreaming of Democracy," *New York Times Magazine*, 2 March 2003, 60.

39. Curt Tarnoff, "The Marshall Plan: Design, Accomplishments, and Relevance to the Present," *CRS Report for Congress* (Washington, D.C.: Congressional Research Service, 6 January 1997), cited in Karin von Hippel, *Democracy by Force: US Military Intervention in the Post–Cold War World* (New York: Cambridge University Press, 2000), 187.

40. Suzanne Goldenberg, "Bush secures Dollars87bn to keep up fight in Iraq: President persuades reluctant US Senate to grant funding as reconstruction takes a back seat to military priorities," *Guardian* (London), 5 November 2003, 15.
41. Robert D. Kaplan, "Supremacy by Stealth: Ten Rules for Managing the World," *Atlantic Monthly*, July/August 2003, 78.
42. One might say that those in power, the warlords and the tribal chiefs, are not without insights of their own. They are sure to see the trend and oppose it. But given the choice between taking them on from the outset, or trying to win them over or buy their cooperation for limited purposes while validating their positions, the second approach is also more attractive to them because, from their viewpoint, the choice is either to give up some power while remaining in place, or face a direct confrontation with the external power.
43. Dexter Filkins, "Chaos and Calm Are 2 Realities for U.S. in Iraq," *New York Times*, 24 August 2003, A1; Michael M. Phillips, "Marines Do It All in One Iraqi City; Now They're Going," *Wall Street Journal*, 22 August 2003, A1.